PETER L. G
President of P
Technology
(PRO-TECH
tional couns
tion firm sp
areas of Just-In-Time,
Quality Control, Automation and Systems Implementation. He was active in the development of Apple Computer's Macintosh Automated Focus Factory in Fremont, CA. Mr. Grieco attended Central Connecticut State University and Wharton School of Finance (Moody's School of Commerce). He serves on the Stanford Research Institute Advisory Board and is a member of the American Society of Quality Control (ASQC) and of the American Production and Inventory Control Society (APICS) and the National Association of Purchasing Manangement (NAPM).

MICHAEL W. GOZZO is co-founder and Executive Vice President of PRO-TECH. His experience covers a wide range — from Director of Manufacturing Operations to Manager of Information Systems. He has worked for both repetitive and discrete manufacturers in aerospace, instrumentation, metals and consumer products. Mr. Gozzo holds a Masters Degree from the University of New Haven (Executive Program) as well as a Bachelor of Science in Finance from the University of Connecticut. He is also a member of ASQC and APICS. In addition, he has lectured for the Connecticut Business and Industry Association, Post College, Boston University and California State University on Management Practices and Information Systems Requirements.

JERRY W. CLAUNCH, C.P.M., Vice President of PRO-TECH, was active in the development and implementation of Just-In-Time at the Kawasaki Motors Corporation, Lincoln, NE. For 20 years, he has been a practitioner and educator in repetitive and discrete manufacturing as well as distribution. Mr. Claunch , who holds degrees from Faith Baptist Bible College and the Computer Programming Institute, serves on the advisory board of the University of Nebraska. He has also served as National Professional Development Chairman for NAPM. In addition, he is a member of ASQC and APICS. He has been a frequent lecturer on JIT and purchasing management for these associations.

Supplier Certification:

Achieving Excellence

Supplier Certification:

Achieving Excellence

PETER L. GRIECO, JR.

MICHAEL W. GOZZO

JERRY W. CLAUNCH

PT PUBLICATIONS, INC.
653 MAIN ST.
PLANTSVILLE, CT 06479

Library of Congress Cataloging in Publication Data

Grieco, Peter L., Jr, 1942-
  Supplier Certification.
  Bibliography; p. 219
  Includes index.
    1. Delivery of goods — United States. 2. Quality of
products — United States. 3. Performance standards.
I. Gozzo, Michael W., 1939-
II. Claunch, Jerry, 1947- . III. Title.
HF5780.U6G75 1988   658.7'2—dc19   88-19706
ISBN 0-945456-02-6

TABLE OF CONTENTS

PREFACE

Supplier Certification is necessary and it will work if we can remember one simple rule: We are all suppliers. If we fail to recognize that a Supplier Certification program has both external and internal aspects, then we will never be able to meet the challenge of domestic and global competition. We will never be able to eliminate the causes of wasted time, money and labor, nor destroy the "Ubiquitous RE-"—rework, repair, reject, refuse— which erodes productivity and profits.

Traditionally, we think of suppliers as companies which deliver products to our plants. They are vendors; they sell their product to us. But, when we think of a supplier as only a vendor, we see only one part of the supply network. There are many other parts as well which other programs neglect. For example, once the product is in our plant, we ship it from department to department, from work station to work station. All these deliveries are also part of the supply network. Finally, once we have manufactured a final product from the various parts and subassemblies shipped to and within our plant, we then supply our customers. A successful Supplier Certification program takes all of these shipments and deliveries into account.

A successful program relies upon the just-in-time delivery of zero-defect material, parts, subassemblies and finished products throughout the supply network. This puts a premium on *making it right the first time*. Thus, the emphasis is on defect prevention, rather than routine inspection. Consequently, the burden of proof will not rest upon inspectors, but on the makers or suppliers of a part. Quality cannot be inspected into a part; it must be there already.

One other piece must also be in place before success can be assured. That piece is top management's commitment to work toward the levels of excellence demanded by Supplier Certification in our own plants. Since many American manufacturers see Supplier Certification as a program only for vendors, top management becomes either surprised or disillusioned by the changes which become necessary in their plants. If we can convince top management to see Supplier Certification as something more than a program imposed upon outside vendors, then there is a real chance to achieve the same levels of quality inside our plants as we demand from our outside suppliers. To accomplish this, however, means that we must also see our outside suppliers not as victims, but as partners in a struggle for excellence which will benefit both.

CREATION OF SUPPLIER PARTNERSHIPS

We need to develop a close relationship with suppliers which is based upon trust and communication. Suppliers will become a part of our organization for the life of the part and the life of the company. These are not "feel-good" statements. As we work together in a partnership to improve quality, we will inevitably find that prices and costs go down for both us and our outside suppliers. Both of us will subscribe to the same specific goals:

- Lower the total cost.
- Strive for smaller lots and frequent deliveries.
- Implement a quality control module.

Quality is the number one issue. Without defect-free parts coming into and being moved around our factories, there is no chance for us to achieve higher levels of efficiency and productivity.

Supplier Certification will also lead to the frequent delivery of smaller quantities of material which will reduce lot sizes, lower inventory levels and reduce Work-In-Process (WIP) levels. These effects on the internal activities of our companies will not work without dramatically better relations with our suppliers. In order for them to meet our frequent delivery schedule and our demand for zero-defect parts, we must be willing to make long-term commitments, share engineering changes, supply them with delivery schedules and exchange product expertise.

One of the points of Supplier Certification is to adjust from the philosophy of ship-to-stock to the philosophy of ship-to-WIP. We must not only get the ordered material to the loading dock, but get it from the loading dock to the shop floor. Supplier Certification will not work if you can't get material to your production lines fast enough to keep them from shutting down. Remember, that in the Supplier Certification environment, there is no excess inventory sitting around that you can use while you wait. Ideally, you should work toward delivering directly to the line, rather than to a receiving area. This will mean making delivery schedules part of the negotiations which lead to a procurement agreement. If a supplier can't guarantee delivery performance, no agreement.

Again, this depends upon good relations with suppliers which are supported by buyer/planners who know our company's material requirements and production schedules so they are able to guarantee stable procurement schedules with suppliers. They should also have the responsibility and authority to structure, enforce and maintain delivery performance.

Ship-to-WIP is the movement of zero-defect material directly to the work station on the production line where it is needed, at just the time it is needed, in the quantity it is needed. It relies on a pull system of manufacturing. When a work station needs a part, it is delivered to the station precisely when it is requested, whether the source is another work station or a supplier. Perhaps the key to ship-to-WIP is to think of certified suppliers as one more work station in a production line. How do you get a supplier to act like one of your own work stations? The answer, of course, is dependent on Purchasing's role in developing good supplier relationships, in making the supplier part of a team.

THE CERTIFICATION PROCESS

In other words, we are trying to achieve quality at the source. But how do we get that quality? By entering into a partnership with a supplier which is based on trust and cooperation. The next question is: How do we get trust, cooperation, and quality from a supplier? The answer is Supplier Certification. We see this as a program in which you can think of yourself as a scientist. You gather facts, make a hypothesis, run your experiment, and use the results to reformulate your hypothesis. The phases in Supplier Certification are similar. Here, too, you gather facts about a supplier, you design quality improvement processes, you put them into practice, and then you audit and maintain the process based on results which you are continuously gathering and interpreting.

In this program, then, you can think of yourself as a medical researcher who takes a patient and not only finds a cure, but finds the means for the patient's continued well-being. You can think of this process as the compilation of a medical history, the implementation of a nourishing diet and a schedule of exercise, and the institution of regular check-ups. Your goal is to develop a healthy supplier, one which will act according to the regimen of TQC (Total Quality Control) and JIT (Just-In-Time).

Supplier Certification is not easy. It requires effort and time. Once completed, it allows for the smooth flow of material, cooperation, communication and, most of all, increased productivity. Quality is the key word — quality of products, information, delivery and counts. Supplier Certification can put you and your suppliers at the leading edge.

One last word. We often speak of ideal situations as though nothing less than their attainment is satisfactory. We won't back down from that demand which we think all American manufacturing companies should place upon themselves. If you have achieved a 95% quality level, strive for 98%. When you reach that level, go for 99%. Once there, go for 99.8%. There is no stopping in Supplier Certification, no resting on your laurels. It is a commitment to the elimination of all waste in your company.

Peter L. Grieco, Jr.
Michael W. Gozzo
Jerry W. Claunch

ACKNOWLEDGEMENTS

With this, our third book, we have firmly established ourselves in the world of business publications. It is through our association with a number of professionals throughout this country and the world that we have witnessed levels of excellence in business. We would like to take this opportunity to thank our clients for their active support of what we call the Total Business Concept. Equally important have been the interactions with some of our consulting staff: Mel Pilachowski, Phil Stang, Mike Stanko, Wayne Douchkoff and Paul Hine. We thank them for their examples, anecdotes and suggestions included in this book.

In particular, we wish to thank C.J. (Chip) Long for his long and continuous support as a Vice President of Professionals for Technology Associates, Inc. We wish him success in the publication of his soon to be released book on Bar Coding.

Another pillar of support has been provided by our capable office staff of Rita, Kevin, Karen and Lesly. In addition, we would like to thank Dick Maccabe who drew the illustrations in this book which aptly grasped and interpreted the text.

As always, we would like to express our appreciation to Steven Marks for his editorial assistance in helping us prepare yet another book in a series which covers today's most urgent quality and manufacturing problems. We hope that your reading will be as pleasurable as our efforts in preparing this book.

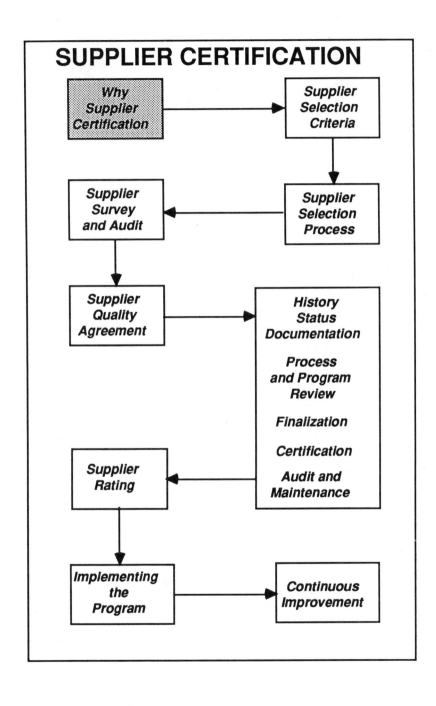

SUPPLIER CERTIFICATION

Why Supplier Certification → **Supplier Selection Criteria**

Supplier Survey and Audit ← **Supplier Selection Process**

Supplier Quality Agreement →

History Status Documentation

Process and Program Review

Finalization

Certification

Audit and Maintenance

Supplier Rating ←

Implementing the Program → **Continuous Improvement**

WHY SUPPLIER CERTIFICATION?

════ 1

Supplier or Vendor Certification is commonly misperceived as a program in which external suppliers guarantee the on-time delivery of zero-defect parts to your plant. In other words, Supplier Certification is a one-way street where you get to pick the direction the traffic takes and the speed at which it travels. The problem with this perception is that it does not allow your own organization to see the internal routes taken by material within your environment. It is highly probable that if an organization views Supplier Certification as a one-way street, then it will soon find itself in the midst of a colossal traffic jam which could threaten the existence and certainly the vitality of the company.

Supplier Certification is both an ***internal*** and ***external*** program. We view a company with its divisions, plants and departments as part of the supplier base. A single part which moves from one operation to another has gone through two supply operations. If you demand that a part shipped by an outside supplier to a machining area be free of defects and on time, then why would you expect any less when it moves from one internal operation to another?

A successful Supplier Certification program demands that the internal flow of material be as orderly as the flow from external suppliers. What is true for the supplier side is also true for the customer side to which you supply finished items. You will be required to view yourself as a certified supplier (on time delivery of quality products in the quantity needed) to internal departments and customers.

Let's define the supplier/customer relationship as the shipment of product from one function to another as the diagram shows:

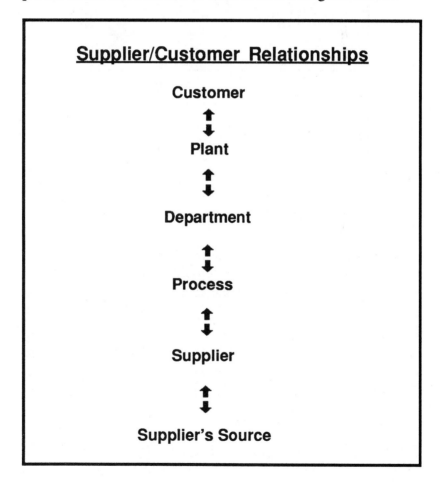

Another view of the supplier/customer relationship is:

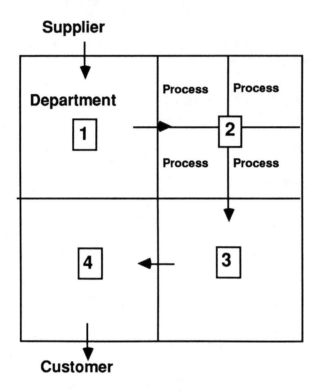

When starting to implement a Supplier Certification program, look at both internal and external sourcing. Internally, this will mean reducing the number of production operations, minimizing queues, reducing set-up times, simplifying product design, evolving toward ship-to-WIP (Work-In-Process) and working toward lot sizes of one. These improvements will eliminate waste and simplify material flow, thus reducing the number and complexity of supply movements.

Externally, a look at sourcing primarily means eliminating the attitude that a large number of suppliers brings security in the form of a consistent flow of material. In reality, that approach is far from the truth. You end up with a supplier network which is out of control and likely to result in logistical nightmares. Shipments from suppliers either come too early or too late and all too often do not adhere to specifications. Since we believe that suppliers won't deliver what we want, we build a system where there are backup suppliers to those who fail for one reason or another. Unfortunately, we perpetuate the problem. Where is the guarantee that the backup suppliers will deliver quality components on time? Now, instead of dealing with one supplier for a particular commodity, we have several, all of whom are equally capable of missing delivery dates, shipping out of specification components or delivering incorrect quantities.

On a recent fact-finding tour of Japan, we asked a production worker what he would do if the single supplier of a part failed to deliver a good product on time. As politely as possible, he answered: "We aren't allowed to think that way." "Why?" we wanted to know. "Our suppliers are all certified," was his reply.

With a reduced base of certified suppliers, there are no early or late shipments or defective parts. A certified supplier delivers quality products on time because the operations of the company are under control. The supplier has done for his or her company what you have done for yours. You both have processes under control.

TIMING OF SUPPLIER CERTIFICATION

Supplier Certification is a process which can take years to complete. We recommend that you do not address all your suppliers at one time and tell them to get their processes under control and then start delivering zero-defect products as you need them. First of all, not all suppliers are capable of this level of excellence. Certainly, you will begin to work first with suppliers which show a commitment to and a capability of working with you as a partner in reaching a level of sustained performance. Second, not all your parts are equally critical to your company. We suggest using Pareto's law to uncover the 20% of your suppliers which account for 80% of the part numbers. Finding the suppliers which are capable of and committed to working with you in a Supplier Certification program has added value. These suppliers will also quickly demonstrate the effectiveness of the program and have the most visible results. Success with them will induce other suppliers to match their results.

These results, however, are difficult to obtain if we view Supplier Certification as a one-way street. It is a two-way street where information about product design, processes and trust travel in all directions. A two-way street raises suppliers from the level of victim to the level of partner. And partners help each other. They share information, eliminate waste and thus reduce total costs together. Shared information will lead the way to long-term agreements between a supplier and a customer.

QUALITY AND THE COMPETITIVE EDGE

Supplier Certification is built upon the roadbed of total quality at each level of the company. The two most important traits you want in a supplier are quality and reliability. Without quality as a way of life, or as a part of the company culture, the two-way street will become riddled with potholes which nobody will be inclined to fix. Quality means never "fixing" or reworking something. It must be built into the product and into all stages of the manufacturing process. Quality focuses on the operator, the process and the product, not on inspection.

Quality is of vital importance to Supplier Certification simply because a defective product or process stops production lines. In a Supplier Certification environment, both process and inventories are brought to a level where "safety" margins are reduced to the lowest possible level. If a shipment arrives in which two out of every 100 are rejected, then a problem exists. Since safety stock doesn't exist, even reworking the parts will affect operations. The time normally spent sorting or reworking components steals time away from operations and throws off the entire production process. Quality is the *oil* which makes the precision components of the Supplier Certification machine function smoothly and in perfect sequence.

Quality means higher profits because it eliminates waste in manufacturing. In short, quality reduces the total cost of a product since it demands that we "do it right the first time" as we pointed out in our first book, *MADE IN AMERICA: The Total Business Concept*. Inventory costs money; lack of a preventive maintenance program costs money; late deliveries cost money; engineering costs money; and so on. The point is that when we add up each element of these costs, we will find the sum to be a considerable percentage of product cost. That number is either subtracted from profits or added to the price of a product. Either way, it will make us less competitive.

Quality, then is the absence of waste. The absence of waste reduces total costs which increases profits as we discussed in our second book, *JUST-IN-TIME PURCHASING: In Pursuit of Excellence*. Over the years, we have looked at the profit equation in the opposite way:

$$Profit = Price - Costs$$

As costs went up, we raised prices to maintain profit levels. From a quality viewpoint (where waste is eliminated), however, the equation looks like this:

$$Price = Profit + Costs$$

In order to maintain profit levels and a competitive price, we need to reduce costs and eliminate waste as defined in both of our previous books.

Waste is:

> Anything other than the absolute minimum level of *material, machines* and *manpower* required to make the product.

Put another way, this definition says that anything or any operation which does not add value to the product is waste. It is obvious that if we eliminate waste, we will increase profits and improve our competitive position. We must streamline our operations in order to exist in a "stockless" environment. To do so, we must first eliminate the problems associated with waste, such as:

> Scrap
> Supplier Delinquencies
> Purchase Lead Times
> Change Orders — Purchasing and Engineering
> Long Set-ups
> Machine Downtime
> Equipment Imbalances
> Inspection Backlog
> Paperwork Backlog
> Absenteeism

How do we tackle these items? They have existed in our companies for a long time. The cost of quality consists of three categories — Appraisal Costs, Failure Costs and Prevention Costs. But that is no excuse for failing to begin quantifying the cost in each of these categories. Determine what they cost now.

Cutting costs, however, can be deceptive as this example shows. Until 1984, a food company sold its product in cans with tin-plated tops. In 1985, the company switched to aluminum tops for a one-time cost improvement of $30,000. Prior to 1984, the company had received only 42 complaints about its product. But, in the three years after 1985, complaints rose to 601, most of them about metal shavings. After spending an additional $300,000 to find the cause of the complaints and how to rectify the problem, the company switched back to tin tops. What looked good from a purchasing objective (Purchase Price Variance) was not effective from a cost of quality perspective or from customer requirements.

As we use Supplier Certification to eliminate failure costs, total costs will go down. Our experience tells us that you can start to have a Supplier Certification program in place in six months, but it takes years to implement fully. If that looms as a formidable task, remember that it doesn't get easier if you begin five years from now when you think you will be in a better position to take on the task. In five years, the only thing that might disappear may be you or your company.

THE GOALS OF SUPPLIER CERTIFICATION

Eliminating waste and inspection are the premier goals of Supplier Certification. Supplier Certification has other important goals which are similar to those of JIT (Just-In-Time) and to TQC (Total Quality Control). Both Supplier Certification and JIT/TQC address the elimination of waste and both have a win/win mentality. What's good for you is good for your supplier. What you expect from your supplier, you should expect from your own company. Supplier Certification works in concert with JIT/TQC.

In fact, it is difficult to think of one without the other because JIT is "the right product in the right place at the right time." Since Supplier Certification demands the same standard as above, it is not surprising that they both have similar goals:

SUPPLIER CERTIFICATION	
GOAL	**ACTION**
Total Quality Control	Ensure that the entire manu-facturing cycle from design review through customer re-ceipt meets quality standards established by the customer.
Quantity	Process and produce the lowest possible quantity by manufac-turing on time. The smaller the quantity, the easier it is to control.
Supplier Partnership	Establish a relationship based on a win/win philosophy.
Logistics	Simplify the control and move-ment of material between func-tions and activities. Incorporate standard objectives.

JUST-IN-TIME/TOTAL QUALITY CONTROL

Unfortunately, many of us believe JIT to be something it isn't. This is why its connection to Supplier Certification is not empha-sized enough.

JIT is <u>not</u>:

> An Inventory Control or Reduction Program.
> A Scheduling Technique.
> A Materials Management Project.

JIT is a concept which integrates the activities between a supplier and your plant, between department and department, and between you and the customer. The three items above are a byproduct of employing the problem-solving philosophy of JIT.

JIT is <u>not</u>:

> A Program for Suppliers Alone.

It is for you and the customer.

JIT is <u>not</u>:

> A New Fad.

It has a long history. Henry Ford used it when he began to mass produce automobiles like the one in the photo on the next page. Deming and Juran taught its principles to the Japanese in the 1950s. JIT is a return to the fundamentals of sound management.

JIT is <u>not</u>:

> A Cultural Phenomenon.

If it was, then why are the Japanese building plants which employ the JIT and Supplier Certification philosophies in America using our workers? We have proven it can be done anywhere.

JIT is <u>not</u>:

> A Program which Displaces Planning.

It evolves out of planning material requirements. JIT coordinates these requirements with the rest of the manufacturing process and suppliers.

JIT is <u>not</u>:

A Panacea for Poor Management.

It is a way of doing business, a management mind-set based on the *Total Business Concept* (TBC) as stated in *MADE IN AMERICA*.

ISSUES, CONCERNS AND OPPORTUNITIES

The Total Business Concept says that we will squarely face issues and concerns as an integrated team and turn them into opportunities. Many people in this country believe that work ethics preclude any attempt to function as an integrated team. We believe that the integration of all levels of management with workers (union and non-union) as well as with suppliers is necessary to a successful implementation. What it really requires is a change in mind-set, in the way we approach problem-solving.

This means that we need to involve everybody in problem-solving from the shipping clerk to design engineering. We must find out what the customer requires and the most efficient way to procure the material needed to build the product. Furthermore, top management must be committed and involved. They must provide focus and direction to the various teams attacking problems in the business. We tend to forget that our people want to contribute their ideas when they feel they will be heard and appreciated.

Companies think of themselves as unique. We are, in terms of having proprietary processes and unique products, but at the most basic level we are all very similar. We procure material, move it, process it and then ship it to customers. Every time we conduct seminars either in the USA or other countries around the world, the same questions come up, whatever the national culture or industry. The most frequently asked questions comes in the form of a negative statement: "Our workers don't have that level of commitment." Our response is that neither did many companies in this country when they embarked upon a Supplier Certification program. Harley-Davidson, for example, was slipping badly before they decided to change their company's mind-set and commitment. They went out and looked at companies that were succeeding. They came back and dedicated themselves to attacking the problems of waste. They were so successful that they asked for government import controls to be removed before they were scheduled to run out.

Another key issue is flexibility. While visiting the Brothers manufacturing plant in Japan on our fact-finding tour of 1988, we were amazed to see various sewing machines, both industrial and commercial, coming down the production line. How was this possible? First, suppliers shipped the right product to the right place at the right time. Second, set-up times for machines were drastically reduced from the levels we see in America. At this plant, it was possible to change an entire line in a matter of minutes. Third, lot sizes were much smaller than those in America. This was possible because it was so easy to set up a machine for another operation. When you take these three improvements into account, the mystique disappears and commitment comes easier since there are visible results.

JIT TRANSPORTATION

Supplier Certification, then, is the management of material and quality both internally and externally. This may present a major logistical problem. You will need to coordinate the activities of a great number of movements of material.

One way to control this movement would be to hire a number of transportation experts to police the movements. This is a superficial solution, however, much like hiring more inspectors in order to improve quality. You need to look at the options and flow of material. You will find that this in-depth look at the underlying causes of material flow and quality will dictate the need to reduce your supplier base. It is far easier to control internal and external supply movements if there are frequent moves being made from fewer sources.

Smaller lot sizes also affect the issue of transportation. Obviously, it is much easier for the supplier to deliver 10 parts on time than 1,000 parts. Supplier Certification works toward lowering the quantities of components and increasing the frequencies of deliveries. There are a number of ways to coordinate the consolidation of deliveries and shipments. You may elect a single consolidation point for a common carrier, send your trucks to a geographical area every day or take advantage of back-haul rates. Standardization of shipping containers can reduce costs and improve accuracy dramatically. Accuracy of count, by the way, is often a hidden cost put into the cost of the material. These efforts will reduce the total cost. Every time you accept a 2% AQL (Acceptable Quality Level), you're paying for two bad parts out of 100. To add insult to injury, you're also paying to have them shipped to you.

A frequent criticism of both JIT and Supplier Certification is that they won't work if your supplier isn't geographically close. Certainly it would be convenient if your suppliers were all next door. It would be like knocking on your neighbor's door to borrow a cup of sugar or a lawnmower. We aren't saying that proximity is not a factor, but that it is a factor you can deal with. At the Apple Macintosh plant in Fremont, CA, for example, we were able to receive products transported by ship from the Orient, 100% on time, all the time. At the Kawasaki plant where Jerry Claunch worked, the experience was the same. Deliveries from Japan were always on time, 100% acceptable and in correct quantities. How? By bringing everybody involved—customs, shipping, receiving—together to discuss how to ensure timely and frequent delivery.

PREVENTIVE MAINTENANCE

A frequently overlooked Supplier Certification issue is preventive maintenance and its effects on manufacturing. In order for Supplier Certification to work, both you and the supplier must have a preventive maintenance program in effect. Furthermore, it must be a scheduled one, not one in which maintenance is done after the fact when the process is already out of tolerance or the work center is down. Also overlooked is the interfacing between a quality control system and maintenance activities. Such aspects of quality control as repair reporting, failure analysis and statistical data accumulation must also be built into the process. This is a function of knowing the characteristics of a machine (bearings, bolts, hoses, etc.) and stopping the process on time for maintenance.

EDUCATION AND TRAINING

Let's review the issue of education and training. There are two questions with which we should be concerned:

- Are time and funding available
  to educate personnel?
- How much would it cost if education
  and training were not implemented?

These costs are often not considered until it's too late. Education and training also require top management commitment. At one of our clients, for example, we conducted a seminar on Supplier Certification which all managers were required to attend.

On the first day, the president states, "I'm 100% behind this program. It's great. It's just what we need, but I can't be here all day. I'll be in and out."

What's the message the personnel are receiving? Is this president truly behind the project? This program won't work if management doesn't show everybody in the room that they are committed. Leaving for meetings throughout the day does not demonstrate commitment.

IMPACT OF ENGINEERING DESIGN

In traditional manufacturing environments, engineering's impact is usually limited to product design. In an environment employing Supplier Certification, Engineering's responsibility extends to the process and producibility. It also extends outside the company to the development of suppliers and customers. Engineering is involved in determining customer needs and designing to that specification. This involvement also includes integrating your company's manufacturing process. The objective is to simplify and reduce the costs of product through design.

There are several reasons why we fail to successfully integrate Engineering into a Supplier Certification program. The main reason is the presence of excessive Bill of Material and process changes. The more changes there are, the more difficult it is to implement Supplier Certification. Changes to a drawing should occur when either product reliability causes a problem in the field or when a change lowers the total cost of the product. That means no more "nice-to-have" changes.

DISCIPLINE

Another reason companies fail is they lack the discipline to make changes in a timely fashion. These changes are not limited to product design, but include process and organizational changes. Nor are they limited to your plant, but include the supplier's as well. Lack of discipline is the absence of a system and methodology to control and support the needs of the organization. This system absence and lack of control results in people not forming a clear picture of their responsibilities and a management that cannot clearly articulate them.

PRODUCT LIFE CYCLES

We also fail when product life cycles are not considered in the planning of various manufacturing activities, such as length of production runs, integration with existing products or supplier availability. When you design a product, producibility is one of the first questions which needs answering. The second question to ask is whether your suppliers can produce the parts you need. You won't find out if they are able to or not by looking at samples provided by suppliers. These samples are always good. We don't know of any companies that send out bad ones. Therefore, you should be looking at your supplier's factory, not its product. Determine for yourself if the supplier has the discipline and levels of productivity to work with you on this product.

DESIGN INTEGRATION

Supplier Certification programs often encounter difficulties because Design has not integrated the following functional groups in the product life cycle:

> Marketing
> Manufacturing
> Quality Assurance
> Engineering
> Purchasing/Materials Management
> Supplier
> Finance
> Customer

One example of a product coming in under the cost design estimate was the Macintosh computer at the Apple plant. They succeeded because everyone was involved in the design right from the beginning. They had a team which selected suppliers based on specific criteria. They knew what to look for in their plants.

PRODUCT TESTING

Many companies also fail to adequately define how a product is to be tested either in the product requirements or the design specifications. The result is that manufacturing does not know how to test a product to achieve the desired results. Instead, we end up establishing test criteria after the product is already in the marketplace. Testing has to be part of the design process. Otherwise, how can we demand zero-defect material from a supplier if we don't know how to test for quality ourselves?

COORDINATION OF ACTIVITIES

One final reason companies fail is because there is a lack of coordination and trust between the supplier and manufacturer. At Progressive Technology, Inc., a tool and die manufacturer in Connecticut, we saw an excellent example of this lack of coordination and trust. Progressive was asked by a customer to build a prototype. After producing one small lot, the company sent the parts to the customer to see if they were acceptable before it produced the remaining 300 parts.

"We can't tell you if the part is acceptable or not," the customer answered back. "The part is in process. Besides, we're not sure if the design we gave you is correct. We're testing the parts, but we can't tell you how."

This way of business has to stop. As we mentioned before, Supplier Certification is a two-way street. If you don't tell your suppliers how to test a part, how can you expect them to build a good one? This is especially true if you don't know whether your prints are correct, which is all too often the case.

RESOURCES REQUIRED

The environment for Supplier Certification requires a *culture change*, a new set of attitudes which reflects a partnership with each supplier. This is accomplished by implementing program requirements at the supplier's as well as at your own plant. Attaining mutual trust will be difficult for American industry whose supplier relations in the past have been decidedly one-sided, but it is not an impossible task. Certainly the best argument for changing your company's attitudes toward suppliers is the program's ability to create a win/win situation for both sides.

One electronics company in this country sees its Supplier Certification program as "a long-term, mutually rewarding business partnership ... in which material quality is assured through open communication, cooperation, design for producibility and functionality, quality planning and effective process control." With this kind of attitude, you can expect to receive high quality parts which could eliminate incoming inspection, lower inventory levels, permit integration of Design and Manufacturing and lessen paperwork. Suppliers, on the other hand, can expect to speed up their cash flow since certified material is accepted upon receipt, to improve their quality levels and to receive more orders since their quality and costs are under control.

With culture change comes the adoption of a ***Total Cost Approach***. As mentioned earlier, a supplier's quoted price is not the true cost of material. Quality and delivery must also be taken into account, but this will mean getting Finance to see beyond the traditional cost systems based on Purchase Price Variance (PPV), Economic Order Quantity (EOQ), machine utilization and the solicitation of three quotes. These systems are outdated. They were derived from the railroad industry in the early years of this century and, as the authors point out in *Relevance Lost*, bear little resemblance to current methods of production. We can no longer be dependent upon price analysis as the major criterion for determining product costs. Cost analysis will have to augment, and even replace, price analysis. This is because cost analysis examines all the costs involved in the manufacturing process, whereas price analysis uses the seller's price without examining the costs and profit which make up the price. A Total Cost Approach is based on the following formula:

Total Cost = Variable Costs + Fixed Costs + Semivariable Costs

The goal is to eliminate overhead allocations as much as possible. A system based on the total cost approach is much more realistic and accountable than traditional approaches for two interrelated reasons. First, the newer approach is based on the Theory of One which says that an operator on a production line only uses as much material as is needed to build to the demand set by the operation in front. Consequently, there isn't any excess material in the plant since only material for which there is a demand is present on the factory floor. Second, what material there is in the plant contributes directly to the production of a finished good, not to inventory carrying costs, not to time lost in receiving areas, not to expediting and not to late materials. Control of material flow is the equivalent of financial control.

LOT SIZING

The control of material is made easier with a *lot-for-lot rule*. We should make only what is sold, produce only the quantity scheduled, store only one container of material on the floor, and so on. Lot-sizing goes hand-in-hand with set-up reduction. On the ideal shop floor, set-ups are so fast that lot sizes of one can be run. To attain levels approaching that ideal requires a persistent effort within your company and with suppliers. A Supplier Certification program has to work toward ensuring the delivery of the right material in the right quantity at the right time. This means frequent, small deliveries directly to the production line in order to reduce inventories. To do so, however, is of no value until the factory floor is weaned from long production runs and large lot sizes in favor of a more *flexible* method of manufacturing.

HUMAN RESOURCES

Another resource required for a successful Supplier Certification program is the cultivation of *generalists*, not specialists. A generalist is better able to see the entire picture, a quality which is almost mandatory in an environment employing the company-wide perspective of Supplier Certification. We are strong advocates of moving people from one department to another as many of the best-run companies in America do. If you have good people in Quality, but they don't know Purchasing, then teach them. Give your people at least one week of training per year in an area they are not familiar with. Good people are hard to find; good people with an awareness of the entire company are even rarer, but necessary to the most successful implementation of Supplier Certification.

CONTROL AND APPLICATION TECHNIQUES

True awareness of an entire company's policies, procedures and operations is not possible without a movement toward *simple control techniques*. The easier it is to explain something, the better the chance of success. The trend toward computerization is somewhat at odds with this requirement. You will have to pay particular attention to the tendency to say that if a computer can't do it, we can't do it. Remember: the Far East has accomplished much of its astonishing gains in quality and productivity without sophisticated computer systems. Many Material Requirements Planning (MRP) programs, for example, have poor Shop Floor Control (SFC) modules which people don't know how to use effectively. Company routings and bills of material are poorly designed. We often complicate the problem by putting these structures on a computer. Now we have computerized chaos instead of control over the basics. The simplest approach is generally the one that works the best.

The same reasoning for selecting simplicity over complexity also applies to the creation of *small work cells*. Whether we call them cells, teams, families, or groups, these units are most effective at problem-solving when they are kept to 6-8 people. Despite the small size, however, they should be given all the tools to make a project happen and should be given profit-and-loss responsibility. This authority and responsibility is instrumental in generating the commitment to drive a Supplier Certification program.

WILL IT WORK?

Success begins with the commitment of your top management and your suppliers' top management to the process of continuous improvement. Top management must be committed to the creation of a company culture which fosters responsibility, authority, vision (company-wide) and accountability. Anything short of this commitment will doom a Supplier Certification program to failure. Middle and lower management as well as direct labor are not about to embark upon a difficult voyage unless they see that their leaders are on board as well. The people who work in our companies will not strive for continuous improvement unless top management has created an environment in which they feel that they can contribute to the company's success and profit.

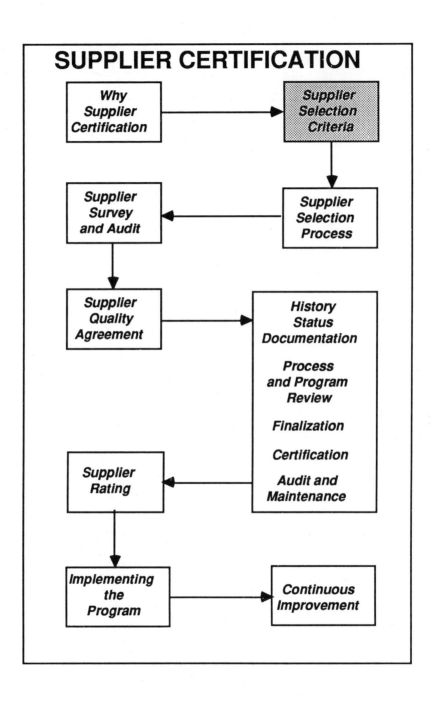

SUPPLIER CERTIFICATION

Why Supplier Certification	→ **Supplier Selection Criteria**

Supplier Survey and Audit ← **Supplier Selection Process**

Supplier Quality Agreement →

- History Status Documentation
- Process and Program Review
- Finalization
- Certification
- Audit and Maintenance

Supplier Rating ←

Implementing the Program → **Continuous Improvement**

SUPPLIER SELECTION CRITERIA

2

The actual criteria you choose to select suppliers will vary according to the size and nature of your business. However, there are criteria which are common to every industry. Therefore, the checklist we have included in this chapter should be used as a guideline. Each company will have to tailor and develop its own checklist. The process of development is extremely important. It is an exercise in creating an integrated approach within your company. With this in mind, let's look in more detail at some of the criteria which are not arranged in any particular order of importance:

SUPPLIER SELECTION CRITERIA

Specifications	Market Involvement
Producibility	Capability
Financial Condition	Supplier's Management Commitment
Geographical Location	Capacity
Quality History	Facilities and Equipment
Customer Base	Labor Conditions
Education and Training	Cost Control
Process and Quality Control	Knowledgeable Sales Force
Competitive Pricing	On-time Delivery
Prior and Post Sales Support	Environmental Programs
Research and Development	Policies and Procedures
Preventive Maintenance	Housekeeping
Ethics	Percent of Business
Subcontractor Policy	Multiple Plants
Organization	Calibration History
Tool Tracking	Quantity

Manufacturing to Specifications

We don't want to send specifications to suppliers for their interpretation. We want them to build the product we specify. To see how well a supplier conforms, look at the number of rejects and the corrective action taken when there are problems. A supplier should be able to answer the following questions:

- When was the last time a corrective action was received from a customer?
- What was done with it?
- How was the corrective action instituted in the supplier's plant?
- How does information about the action get fed back to the customer?

Producibility

Can the supplier make the part to specification? And, in the quantities needed? Can the supplier take a design and produce the part consistently in a cost-effective manner?

Financial Condition

Be careful about what information is used to make judgments in this category. We recommend using a "10K" because it goes into more detail than other financial reports. If the supplier is a private company, it may be difficult obtaining financial information unless the Chief Financial Officer is willing to share it. A supplier willing to share information demonstrates openness and an ability to be a partner.

Geographical Location

Our rule is that we should make every effort to do business with companies (approved by the team) who are within 60 minutes of our plant, whether that's by truck, rail, airplane or boat. There will be exceptions, of course, but this rule should be in place to limit the areas in which we should search for suppliers. This brings procurement under the umbrella of a Supplier Certification program. Furthermore, we recommend that any supplier outside the 60-minute radius be accepted by a certification team. This is to avoid other functional areas developing their own sources without looking at local suppliers.

Quality History

Besides checking with previous customers of suppliers, it is also important to check for quantitative data which substantiates quality. Don't rely on vague statements that the supplier is committed to quality. Look for evidence of quality throughout the supplier's facility.

Customer Base

Know the supplier's customer base for two reasons:

> • To check for references.
> • To see if they are doing business as
>   partners with other corporations.

Education and Training

A supplier who has an extensive education and training program is one already committed to continuous improvement. These are the companies we want to buy from because our own Supplier Certification program will fit neatly into their plans. The basic question we want answered is how many hours per week of training do workers and management get in areas such as Statistical Process Control (SPC), material management, purchasing, set-up reduction, etc.? A supplier with well-rounded employees, who have a complete picture of their company, is one that will help the most. Another question we might ask to determine the extent of their education and training is what does the supplier do when it hires a new worker. Are they thrown right into their job? Or, as in the early stages of the Macintosh plant in Fremont, CA, does the company orient all new hirees (management and production) to the product by having them spend a week on a mock production line building the product? The rationale is that when it comes time to make a decision, an employee is better equipped to decide correctly having undergone hands-on experience. In such an environment, for example, a buyer would not be ignorant of the quality tests performed on the product he or she is buying.

Process and Quality Control

Another label for this category is Statistical Process Control (SPC). As noted before, process and quality control is critical. We want to select suppliers who will allow us to look at their process routing sheets and documentation. Does the company make the product as the sheet indicates? If it does, then we can be more sure that the process is under control. If the route sheet is inaccurate, then we should begin to question the degree of process control. Certification is difficult without process control.

Competitive Pricing

Quite simply, are the supplier's prices competitive with those of its competition? Competitive pricing is not the answer if it is based on a "three-bid" mentality.

Prior and Post Sales Support

Besides the presence of warranties, guarantees and replacement parts, we should also look for suppliers who are committed to solving problems before and after a sale is made. Obviously we want to avoid the fly-by-night companies which disappear after a delivery is made. Here, too, we can look at the history of a supplier's performance with other customers.

Organization

Although the emphasis here is on the presence of well-organized quality and material departments, the same criteria apply to the company as a whole. Basically, we should be looking for the difference between organization and bureaucracy. We can determine which state exists by observing how many levels of management the supplier has; whether information flows as it is designated or whether an informal grapevine exists; or, by questioning all levels about their understanding of quality. A well-organized company is a well-informed company whose operations are streamlined to eliminate waste.

Preventive Maintenance

Look for three particular conditions:

- Preventive maintenance on a regular, standard schedule.
- Service while machines are running.
- Scheduled stops in the process for maintenance.

Ethics

Suppliers should subscribe to and follow all Good Manufacturing Practices (GMP) and obey all laws and regulations they are subject to. Our philosophy is that you can't teach ethics, employees must be ethical.

Subcontractor Policy

Suppliers should divulge whether or not they use subcontractors. Obviously, such subcontractors must be able to produce to your specification if they are shipping parts to a company which will supply you in turn. If your supplier does use subcontractors, you should know how they source these companies and how much control they have over their process. One weak link in the chain of the suppliers can weaken the entire Supplier Certification program. Subcontractors should be avoided, if at all possible.

Research and Development

Suppliers that have aggressive and innovative R&D departments, as evidenced by the number of patents they have, are most desirable. They are the companies that will grow with you, that are open to new ideas and new ways to cut costs. This same innovative attitude should extend beyond the research department and should be a consequence of management commitment to continuous improvement.

Tool Tracking

Part of process control is tool tracking since bad tools make bad parts. A supplier should know how many parts have been produced off of any tool and what is the life of that tool. Tools should also be on a regular maintenance schedule and be replaced before they begin making bad parts. Suppliers who eke out a few more strokes from a tool to cut costs are being penny wise and pound foolish. These are not the suppliers we want for our program. If the tool life exceeds what was planned, that is acceptable; if the tool is used beyond its life limits, that's not acceptable.

Market Involvement

Here we look to buy from suppliers that view the material we procure as their main line of business. As a participant at one of our seminars put it: "If you want to print a hard-cover book, you don't go to a printer who specializes in spiral-bound covers." Ideally, we would like to do business with an industry leader that is at the forefront of any technological advances. These are the suppliers who can advise us best about the producibility of the product we want to build. In effect, this category directs us to the experts.

Capability

Is the supplier adequately and correctly staffed for machines and manpower? Does it have methods in place which make it capable of producing parts to specifications?

Supplier's Management Commitment

This category is a consequence of all the other categories. It is likely that the presence of process and quality control means that management is committed. A truly committed management assigns responsibility and authority to all levels of the company and expects them to be accountable for their areas.

Capacity

We don't want a supplier that runs its machines 100% of the time. Nor do we want a supplier that puts on extra shifts during peak periods. We want a steady state: 80% capacity with time for preventive maintenance and problem-solving. We can't implement Supplier Certification with a supplier that does not allow an operator to shut down a machine until it finally breaks down. One way to see whether this happens or not is to ask the operator. Let the operator show you how the machine gets calibrated and maintained and how frequently.

While we are on the subject of machine maintenance, we don't advocate having a special shift just for preventive maintenance workers. Operators should do some maintenance themselves and it should be scheduled by the Planning Department as a work order. The problem with a special shift is that the maintenance workers don't talk with the operators who know the most about the machines.

Facilities and Equipment

We should not look only for new equipment and facilities. What will the equipment and facility look like six months from now, or one year? This is the question we want answered. A good supplier manages and maintains all its equipment whether it is old or new. In fact, well-maintained older equipment could be a sign of a better managed company than brand new equipment.

Labor Conditions

Whether the supplier has a union or non-union shop, the company should have good relations with its people. We have worked with both types of companies and we have found that when employees are treated with respect and listened to, they will build quality parts. Not only that, but they will help their company continuously improve to build still better parts at more cost-effective prices. Supplier Certification relies on this type of participation to be effective itself.

Cost Control

Under this category, we should look for suppliers that are willing to work with us in breaking down the components of cost: material, labor, overhead, profit, transportation, etc. This is a prelude to a whole program of total cost measurement and subsequent waste elimination undertaken by both you and the supplier.

Knowledgeable Sales Force

Knowing prices is not enough. A supplier's sales force should know the answers to questions you have about the process, machine capability and methods. Avoid suppliers that use their sales force as merely order-takers.

On Time Delivery

Look for a record of timely delivery by checking references and other customers. Remember that on time delivery does not mean delivering early. That is just as detrimental to a Supplier Certification program as is late delivery. On time delivery means 100% on time, every time.

Environmental Programs

When a supplier is regulated by environmental agencies, be sure that it has control over any methods and procedures used for getting rid of hazardous wastes, etc. Failure to comply with government regulations is a violation of the law and we should avoid companies practicing bad business.

Policies and Procedures

In a way, this is the crux of Supplier Certification. There is one simple question to ask here: Are policies and procedures being followed at the supplier's plant? Or, do they just sit on a shelf?

Housekeeping

An example from one of our fact-finding tours of the Far East best demonstrates what we mean here. At a factory we visited in Japan, the floors were so clean you could eat off of them. The management at this company told us this was because they wanted to see when a machine started to leak oil. Then, they would know that it needed immediate attention. Housekeeping in Japan is part of Preventive Maintenance. This is not usually the practice here in America. When a machine leaks, we put a drying compound on the floor to soak up the oil. We don't see it as a sign of a problem. We tend to live with it and don't fix the machine until it finally breaks down. Housekeeping means everything has a place and everything is in its place as the photo on the opposite page shows.

Percent of Business

An objective of the program is never to be more than 35-40% of a particular supplier's business in terms of dollars or parts because that could put the company out of business if you were to cut your orders or end them. We had a client who initially shipped almost 100% of its products to the computer industry. We warned him that if this industry slumped, his company might fail. Since the company was in the plastic injection molding business, we suggested it develop a business plan in which it would sell 20% of its products to the automotive industry, 40% to the computer industry, 20% to the toy industry and 20% to the cosmetic industry. Now, even if the company were to lose a third of its business, it would not fail. It may not make a profit in the interim, but at least it would be around to find more business. When selecting suppliers to be certified, find ones who will not fall over if one leg of their business is pulled out from beneath them.

Multiple Plants

If a supplier has more than one plant, then it really is more than one supplier. This means that we must certify each of the plants if they all participate in supplying material to us. Otherwise, we run the danger of getting parts from the plant which does not have its process under control.

Calibration History

This area is similar to tool tracking. We need to look for evidence that gauges and fixtures are maintained and calibrated on a regular schedule. We don't want to see calibration done only when bad parts are produced.

Quantity

Does the supplier deliver in the quantities ordered? We cannot allow the established tolerances of +/- 10%. We only want what we need; no more, no less.

HOW TO USE THE CRITERIA

The highlights above indicate the creative ways we can assess a supplier. Although there are over 25 categories listed, most companies look at less than half when they select a supplier. Traditionally, companies give a small order to a new supplier and look at their performance before deciding whether to issue more purchase orders. But since first orders are almost always perfect, companies start to depend on more subjective criteria. For example: "I feel good about this supplier" or "I think he'll do a good job."

We must move away from this "feel-good" process of selecting suppliers. Once we have drawn up a list of criteria, our next step is to clean up the categories so there is no duplication and write a self-explanatory paragraph which describes what we are seeking. Then, assign a point value to each so that the categories add up to a total of 100 points. Now, we can determine where to draw the line for those suppliers which qualify. The qualifying score can vary, but it should be 70 or better. Note that if a supplier ships two different classes of material, it must qualify for each commodity.

Scoring suppliers requires an on-site survey, but you can't do that without an objective checklist of criteria. Determining that criteria is the most important part of the Supplier Selection process, only just ahead of involving a multi-disciplined team.

In the past, companies have selected suppliers haphazardly. Typically, buyers are hurried in the task of finding suppliers. They base their decision on a sample first order or by allowing Engineering to sidestep the procurement process and select suppliers without input from other members of the selection team. A goal of Supplier Selection is to shrink the supplier base. Allowing departments to use any method not based on objective criteria will have the opposite effect. We know of one semiconductor company which set a goal of shrinking its supplier base from 1,000 to 750. But, since it failed to bring the program together under a team given the task of drawing up selection criteria, the supplier base had grown to 1,340 by the year's end!

We must have a team to select suppliers. This team should consist of representatives from Purchasing, Engineering, Manufacturing, Finance, Quality Assurance, etc. They should gather information from as many sources as possible in order to make their selection decision. These sources can be professional societies, marketing contacts, the Thomas Register and past experience. Then, the team sits down and votes on which suppliers are potentially certifiable. This decision depends upon how many suppliers we need for each product and commodity. It may be that we need two suppliers for sheet metal and two for injection molding when we start the program. We may be able to lower this figure as the program gets underway. We don't want to move too quickly, however. We don't want to set a goal of dropping from 500 suppliers to 100 if that endangers our comfort level.

WHO SHOULD YOU SELECT TO WORK WITH FIRST?

Frequently, clients ask us "Which suppliers should we work with first?" We always tell the story of Tom Malone at North American Tool and Die Company who was recently highlighted in Tom Peter's book, *THRIVING ON CHAOS*. When Tom started his company, he targeted 25 companies he wanted to do business with. One of these companies was Digital Equipment Corporation where one of us, Peter Grieco, was working at the time as the Materials Director. Malone calls up Digital one day and says, "I'm not looking for any orders. I would like a half-hour of your time so you can define what you want from a supplier."

We make an appointment to list what Digital wants from a supplier. A month later, we receive a follow-up call.

"I recently completed a business plan. Will you take an hour to critique it?" I tell him I would be glad to look it over and make some comments for him. A month later, he calls again.

"I wrote a final draft of my business plan. Will you look at it?"

By now, I can't refuse. I'm interested in what he's doing. I look at it, make some comments and send it back. Two weeks later, it's Tom Malone on the phone again.

"Can I have an order to see if my plans work?"

I can't say "no." I'm hooked. We've worked together for the past two-and-a-half months and developed a relationship. That's the type of supplier you want to work with first: one who is concerned with doing it right the first time.

In selecting suppliers, we can choose among several options or alternative factors:

1. **Best Supplier/Products**
2. **Worst Supplier/Products**
3. **Highest Dollar/Volume Items**
4. **Lowest Dollar/Volume Items**
5. **Pareto's Law**
6. **Bulky Items/Large Space Concerns**
7. **Frequent Delivery**

APPROVED, QUALIFIED AND CERTIFIED VENDOR LISTS

There are a limited number of suppliers who have Tom Malone's qualities at the outset of the certification process. We must work with potential suppliers to raise them to the level of partnership. Companies generally have vendor lists which identify those suppliers which meet certain criteria. These lists are known today as the Approved Vendor List (AVL), Qualified Vendor List (QVL) and Certified Vendor List (CVL).

The AVL is the list of suppliers that a company can buy from now or has bought from in the past. Being on the list does not mean that the supplier ships material which meets all engineering requirements. In fact, the material can range from good to poor. The criteria today for getting on the AVL is very simple: the supplier has previously been given a purchase order and now has an account number on our records. This alone makes a supplier eligible to buy from.

The QVL is the list of suppliers that meet specifications which were established earlier. Their material is rarely rejected and they perform satisfactorily in a high percentage of the areas in the Supplier Selection criteria. They are the cream of the crop, the suppliers we want to work with and the ones we think can end up on the Certified Vendor List.

All too often, however, the QVL is not what it should be. Let's say Purchasing needs to buy a new product. One of the suppliers on the AVL manufactures the needed part, but it has not been qualified for the part. The company is not on the QVL. Normally, Purchasing would need authorization from Quality before it could buy the part. Quality would do a survey to see if the parts conform to requirements, but it often doesn't because there isn't enough staff and the company needs the part right away. So what happens is that the supplier gets put on the QVL without a survey.

Such fuzzy definitions of the AVL and QVL make it easy for a

supplier to move up a notch. A QVL rating should be the result of an objective process, one in which the supplier meets at least 60-70% of the supplier selection criteria. This is as true for medium or low technology companies as it is for hi-tech ones. The item that will shut down a production line is the bracket bought from a supplier that moved from the AVL to QVL without a rigorous appraisal.

The decision to be put on the QVL must be made by the same team responsible for the selection process. Including somebody on the

QVL must be a conscious, not an unconscious, process. We need to go through the whole vendor list and separate the non-inventory items. Then, let the buyers break down the vendor list into the AVL and QVL categories. When a supplier of a certain part makes the QVL, then stop buying that part from suppliers on the AVL. The QVL supplier is the candidate for a long-term partnership and eventual certification.

WHAT ABOUT DISTRIBUTORS?

Many of us don't buy directly from manufacturers, but from distributors. How can we control the selection of suppliers in this situation? If we're a high volume buyer, we can exert control over the distributor's choice of suppliers. If we aren't a high volume buyer, then we should make every effort to find distributors which are selective and have a good reputation. Perhaps the best idea, however, is to show our Supplier Certification program to our distributors so that they can select better suppliers themselves. The rewards are self-evident. If they buy from better suppliers, they will get better parts and thus get more business. In essence, this is the same evidence of mutual benefits that we showed to our own suppliers. Our objective is to work only with suppliers who can be certified at some point in the future. In the next chapter, we will show you how to survey your suppliers to find out which ones meet your criteria.

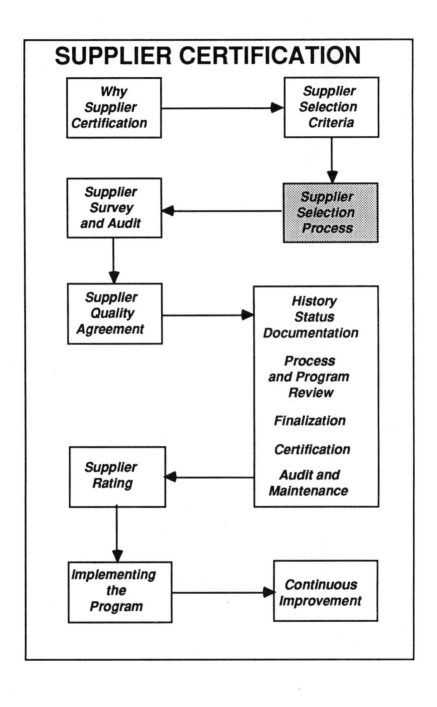

SUPPLIER SELECTION PROCESS

 **3**

Changing the one-way street of supplier relations to a two-way street means there will be new directions in the way we select suppliers. The one-way street of the fifties, sixties and early seventies was marked by a signpost which looked like this:

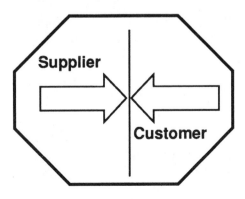

"Adversary" Supplier Relations

This was the era of adversarial relations in which customers made demands upon suppliers without extensive consultation in order to build an understanding between the two parties. By the late seventies, however, customers began to notice that this relationship had serious shortcomings. It was never entirely clear who was supposed to do what and when, so a new era was ushered in marked by this signpost:

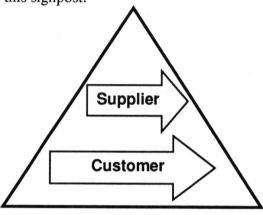

"Contract" Supplier Relations

The contract era of supplier relations lasted well into the eighties and, as the sign shows, did point both parties in the same direction. Contract administrators, or lawyers, were hired in procurement functions to review contracts so there would be no ambiguity about how customers would work with suppliers. What this era still left out was continual contact with the supplier to work on building a partnership. This is the work of the new era of supplier relations which will be marked by a transition to a signpost which looks like the one on the following page.

The partnership era shows both arrows side by side and pointing upwards as the supplier and manufacturer work together to improve quality, delivery, performance and cost. Thus, the first question we should ask suppliers today is: Are you willing to become our partner in eliminating waste and embarking upon a continuous improvement process?

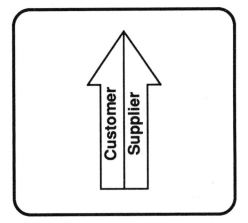

"Partnership" Supplier Relations

THE SIGNS OF PARTNERSHIP

Along the "partnership" highway, there will be several other signs which indicate the general direction taken in your own company and in your supplier's operation.

The first sign will be a clear *commitment* to quality by management at all levels of the organization.

The second sign will state the need for *visible/measurable* quality programs available to all personnel in both internal and external companies about to enter into a partnership. These types of programs mean that achieved results are plotted against the objectives and goals to track performance of the program.

The third sign will mark embracing a *zero-defect* philosophy which states "do it right the first time" and that a company does not accept continued rejects at any point in the process.

The fourth sign, *on time delivery*, demands the arrival of material when it is required and not before or after. The objective is to use material as soon as it hits the receiving dock (Ship-To-Stock) and eventually to have material shipped directly to the line (Ship-To-WIP). This will be greatly helped, of course, by the adoption of standard packaging which will eliminate the need for counts.

THE SUPPLIER SELECTION TEAM

The task of a manufacturer is to develop an open and trusting relationship with the supplier. The first step in selecting partners is *not* to designate one department as being solely responsible for selection. You will have difficulty entering into a partnership with a supplier if you haven't established that a partnership exists between the departments within your company.

The supplier selection team should be composed of representatives from at least the following departments:

> Engineering — design, manufacturing, industrial, etc.
> Manufacturing — operations, process
> Purchasing — international, domestic, commodity
> Finance — cost accounting
> Quality — vendor quality engineer, manager

There are various techniques available in starting this type of program. For new start-up programs, selection is a far easier process. When developing a new factory, there is an excellent opportunity to select suppliers for a new plant and product from their inception. Most companies, however, need to first review their existing supplier base and then rank them in an order which distinguishes between good and bad performers. When reviewing the supplier base to determine a reasonable number that we can work with in an efficient and productive manner, we can apply Pareto's law to the existing supplier base. Pareto's law says that 20% of your suppliers account for 80% of your procurement costs.

Commodity	SKU	Present # of Suppliers	Required # of Suppliers	Supplier Meeting Req't	Required New Suppliers
Plastics					
Sheet Metal					
Molded					
Cables					
Electronics					
Totals					

Commodity Code and Product Type Chart

Another approach is to determine, by commodity codes and product types, how many suppliers are required by category and in aggregate.

In this manner, we can determine from the chart on the previous page how many of our existing supplier base we will retain and how many new ones we need. The selection team will have to address this issue as a first step in the selection process.

The supplier selection team's next task, now that the supplier base is reduced, is to establish supplier selection criteria. Each member of the team brings expertise to the task which together adds up to a whole greater than the sum of its parts. *Engineering*, for example, is responsible for product design and whether the design for an existing product can be simplified. In conjunction with *Manufacturing*, it should also be determining whether the product is being efficiently produced. Manufacturing, along with *Quality*, is responsible for process control both in the plant and at the supplier's. Remember that we cannot inspect for quality, it must be built into the product through the effective control of both design and the manufacturing process. *Purchasing*, of course, smooths the way for good supplier relations in which zero-defect parts are always delivered on time. Lastly, *Finance* needs to be on the team to ensure that outdated purchasing measurements and practices like Purchasing Price Variance (PPV) and Economic Order Quantity (EOQ) are replaced by new procedures reflecting company-wide measurements and a Total Cost approach. In addition, they supply the required financial data about the supplier to the team.

REQUIREMENTS OF A CERTIFIED SUPPLIER

The supplier selection team's next task is to determine what the basic requirements are to become a certified supplier and the key questions to ask when selecting a supplier. A high technology electronics company recently defined its requirements as:

1. Average reject rate less than 5%.
2. Average delinquency rate less than 10%.
3. Willingness to produce parts to center of specification range as demonstrated by Statistical Process Control charts.

These are certainly good goals although they aim too low and don't place an emphasis on continuous improvement. Without a JIT/TQC philosophy, there is little assurance that the goals above can be attained or maintained.

WHAT ARE THE GOALS?

The first requirement a potential certified supplier must meet is that its philosophy agrees with yours and that you share similar goals. You can detect this by exploring a potential supplier's relationships with its own suppliers. A supplier must have a quality control system in place which subscribes to the same zero-defect goals and process controls as your company does. This does not exclude suppliers who fail to meet these requirements initially, but to exclude them from the first forays into a Supplier Certification program. We can't afford to waste time and money on suppliers which either accept poor quality or don't want to enter into a partnership.

Another key requirement is a satisfactory answer from suppliers to the question of dedicated capacity. We advocate that a supplier schedule capacity at only 80% in order to leave time for preventive maintenance, emergency situations, flexibility and problem-solving. Given that, an objective is to "regularize" the production schedule so that it can be expressed as a daily requirement. We want suppliers who are flexible enough to make what we want when we want it. If you need 10 parts today and eight parts tomorrow, then you receive 10 parts today and eight tomorrow.

Another criterion is suppliers who are capable of entering into long-term agreements for 3-5 years or the life of a product. In these agreements, it is stipulated that both you and the supplier will work together on:

> Product Cost Reduction
> Quality and Specifications
> Value Engineering
> Total Cost Reduction

These agreements can be executed as a system contract or blanket order as long as several criteria are established:

> **1. The production forecast will fluctuate based on customer demand.**
>
> **2. Criteria will be in place indicating how to add or subtract from capacity in order to "regularize" the production schedule as a daily requirement.**
>
> **3. A ceiling on how much material we are responsible for if the criteria is not met.**

Such a system may work like this:

Every month, you call the supplier with a rolling one-year forecast for that item. You can then change the quantity for one day's production as the following chart shows:

Days	% Change
0-30	+/-20%
31-60	+/-50%
61>	+/-100%

In this system, you are only responsible if the production schedule changes beyond the parameters for 30 days of raw material, 14 days of Work-In-Process and 0 days of finished goods. This insures that the supplier is producing Just-In-Time and not filling up warehouses with products we may not need.

Another key requirement is the synchronization of daily production and deliveries with the production schedule. The biggest obstacle to achieving this is long lead time. Of the five elements of lead time (queue, set-up, run, wait and move), queue time accounts for 80-90% of the total time. Thus, we have immediate control over a major portion of lead time by reducing lot sizes and employing a pull system in which both we and the suppliers only build a product when there is a demand for it.

We have been lulled into thinking a supplier's lead time is unchangeable. A few years ago, we remember that suppliers of ball bearings announced that their lead time would double from 4-8 weeks to 8-16 weeks. The planners and buyers at manufacturing companies then doubled their orders so they would not run out of bearings. Faced with this sudden surge in demand, the suppliers doubled their lead time again within a relatively short period of time. The buyers then doubled their orders again. Before we knew it, the lead time had grown to 82 weeks. In order to bring some order back to this chaotic development, we decided to offer one of the suppliers a total dollar per month purchase order. We didn't know what we wanted next week, let alone next year, but we informed the supplier that we would tell him our forecast at the beginning of each month. Only under this agreement were we able to shrink lead time.

We often complicate supplier relations more than necessary. In part, this is because we do not truly listen to what customers want. At one of our seminars, a participant asked us what he could do about lead time when the paper he needed was only produced twice a year in quantities of 200,000 pounds. It may have been possible to arrange delivery with an agreement just described, but we had an easier solution.

"Why does it have to be this stock of paper?" we asked. "Why can't you use a stock that is produced more often and in smaller quantities?"

He hemmed and hawed for a while and then told us that his company had to use that particular paper "because that's what the graphic artists said we needed."

"What does the customer want?" we asked. "Do they need this paper? Do they really care whether the paper is the fancy French vanilla variety or just the plain vanilla?"

It turned out that once the specifications were reviewed, the customers didn't care one way or another.

A Supplier Certification program is a long-term commitment. Too many American company executives are trying to turn their programs into 3-6 month projects. They don't understand that continuous improvement takes time. They also forget that the programs and buying practices of the past have not worked. A culture change is required at all levels of the supplier's and customer's plants.

Others think that it is possible to develop the program in one plant at a time. We advocate a Total Business Concept. In order to do this, all plants must be treated as suppliers which should meet the same criteria as external suppliers. If sister plants don't meet a specific guideline, then the use of their material is unacceptable. Such a condition requires complete corporate commitment to quality and supplier certification.

The last key requirement for becoming a certified supplier is the existence of a complete process and quality control system. The supplier quality standards of Baxter Travenol Laboratories, Inc. require that "Statistical Process Control should be an integral part of the supplier's operation." Such a system, the standards say, is "necessary during manufacturing operations to monitor and control processes, prevent the manufacture of large quantities of defective parts, provide uniformity, and to identify when corrective action is necessary." We promote its emphasis on "process acceptance rather than product acceptance." The goal of Supplier Certification is to eliminate Incoming Inspection and to ship material directly to the line precisely when and where it is needed. This is only possible when you can be sure that the supplier not only has quality and process controls in place, but a system which maintains those controls.

PRESENTING THE PROGRAM TO THE SUPPLIER

Up to this point, we have discussed the basic requirements of a certified supplier. Now let's look at how to involve suppliers in the certification process. Obviously, we can't start making demands on companies, otherwise suppliers will see themselves as "victims" of your program. An approach is to plan a supplier symposium in which the benefits of Supplier Certification are presented to suppliers who were selected based on how many suppliers are needed.

SUPPLIER SYMPOSIUM

Once these suppliers are selected, we should hold a supplier symposium according to the sample agenda on the next page. Each member of the supplier certification team is required to present a portion of the program. This should be done in an integrated manner so that the presentation demonstrates what Supplier Certification means to your business and theirs.

AGENDA
PROGRESSIVE TECHNOLOGY
SUPPLIER SYMPOSIUM

LOCATION: Corporate Offices, Plantsville, CT
DATE: January 15, 1989

9:00 - 9:30	Arrival of Suppliers Coffee and Pastries
9:30 - 9:45	Introductory Remarks — Supplier Interfaces with Design, Purchasing, Quality, Production and Finance
9:45 - 10:00	Opening Remarks and Review of Objectives by President
10:00 - 10:30	Ship-to-Stock vs. Ship-to-WIP — the Role of Inspection
10:30 - 11:00	Non-Conforming Product and Corrective Action System
11:00 - 11:30	How to Attain 100% Accuracy
11:30 - 12:00	Process Control of Manufacturing Operations
12:00 - 1:00	Lunch
1:00 - 1:30	Do It Right the First Time — Design and Suppliers
2:00 - 2:30	Quality Control
2:30 - 2:45	Coffee Break
2:45 - 3:00	Preventive Maintenance
3:00 - 3:30	Total Cost Approach to Supplier Certification
3:30 - 4:00	Management Issues and Concluding Remarks

The president of your company should talk about competition and how it is forcing us to develop less adversarial relationships with suppliers. Indeed, the president will want to stress that a partnership is the most sensible and mutually beneficial approach to take.

The Quality team member will talk about what that department expects from suppliers. Purchasing would then discuss the criteria the company will use to select suppliers and the process of how it intends to certify them. The presentation may conclude with Manufacturing announcing that your company will practice what it is preaching by starting an internal program addressing the very same requirements.

A supplier's salespeople are not the intended guests of this symposium. We are looking for people who have the authority to buy into the process, people such as the company president, general manager, engineering department head and quality department head. The principal message of the symposium is that we are going to work together. Therefore, once your company's speakers give this message throughout the day-long meeting, you're committed to following through. The worst thing to do is stir the pot and then let it sit on the back burner. What supplier would ever trust you again? You must demonstrate a commitment to the program before you can expect suppliers to buy in.

In the final analysis, a symposium not only describes the supplier certification program to potential participants, but acts as another step in the winnowing process. At the end of the symposium, there should be some time set aside to sign up those who are interested in joining the effort. Once you have shown your commitment to the program, it is time for the suppliers to show theirs.

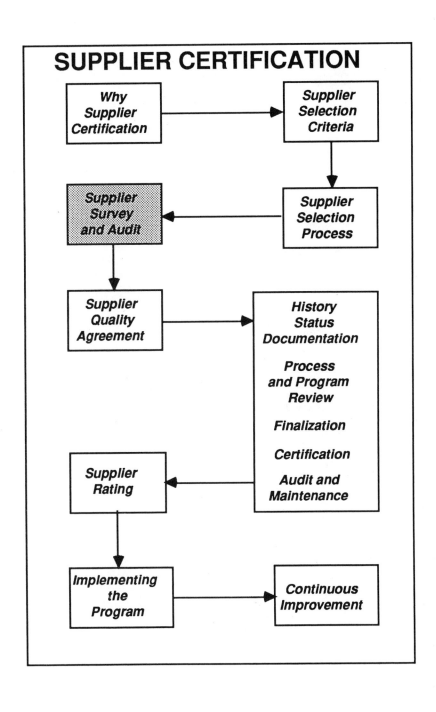

SUPPLIER CERTIFICATION

Why Supplier Certification	**Supplier Selection Criteria**
Supplier Survey and Audit	**Supplier Selection Process**
Supplier Quality Agreement	**History Status Documentation** **Process and Program Review** **Finalization** **Certification** **Audit and Maintenance**
Supplier Rating	
Implementing the Program	**Continuous Improvement**

SUPPLIER SURVEYS AND AUDITS

$$\overline{}\mathbf{4}$$

If the first part of the Supplier Certification journey is learning the JIT/TQC mind-set and preparing a list of supplier selection criteria, then the second part is surveying suppliers to find out whether they meet them. The criteria developed in the last chapter forms the basis of surveys.

In general, the criteria look for two things — the presence of a sound quality system and a manufacturing process which is under control. In particular, we judge suppliers in eight major areas. These also form the basis for supplier audits. One of the more frequent questions asked is: "What is the difference between a supplier survey and a supplier audit?" In its simplest terms, a

SURVEY CRITERIA

Quality Management

Design Information

Procurement

Material Control

Manufacturing Control

Final Inspection

Calibration

Quality Information

survey of a supplier is done before it manufactures a product. The survey determines what is happening at the supplier's plant. An audit, on the other hand, is done after a supplier begins making a product. Its purpose is to assure us that what we want to happen is, indeed, happening at the supplier's plant. A survey is used to find a supplier capable of producing zero-defect parts which will be shipped on time. An audit can be thought of as a maintenance tool, whereby we check to see that the supplier's quality and manufacturing processes remain under control. An audit can also be used as a method to improve a supplier's performance by pointing out weaknesses. It can point out areas where more education and training is needed.

MANAGEMENT MATURITY LEVELS

The first indicators of a supplier's potential to be certified are company-wide in nature — management commitment and organizational status. These elements, of course, can also be used to determine your own management maturity levels. Let's look first at the levels of understanding and attitude.

At the first level, a company's management has no comprehension whatever of supplier certification, Just-In-Time or Total Quality Control. At the second level, management is aware of what must be done, but has committed no dollars to the program. As money is added, management rises to the third level in which it is willing to learn and support expansion of Supplier Certification programs. At the fourth level, management is actively participating in quality and manufacturing control programs. The suppliers of level four companies are actively involved with quality in this process. The fifth level is the goal that both we and our suppliers want to attain. At this level, management sees Supplier Certification as an integral part of its company.

Both the status of the company as a whole and the status of its quality organization go hand-in-hand with management maturity levels. The chart on the next page shows the characteristics of a company at each of the five levels.

We should be looking for suppliers who rank in Level 3 to Level 5 on all three scales. As you can see, there is some measure of management commitment at this level and this commitment is essential to the success of a Supplier Certification program.

Levels	Management Traits	Quality Organization	Company Status
1	Lack of understanding	No inspector present	Unaware of what causes poor quality
2	Sees value of change, but no commitment of money	Firefighting mode; symptoms treated, not causes	Constant quality problems are present
3	Willing to change, support and learn	Management becomes involved in prevention	Commitment to continuous improvement
4	Management is participating	Quality effectively controls process	Shift to defect prevention
5	Management is part of improvement team	Zero-defects is the only acceptable method	Supplier certification is a way of life

EVALUATION METHODS

Ranking suppliers on a scale must be as objective as possible. We do this by assigning a point value to each criterion. By all means, we must stop asking this question:

DON'T ASK: Do I feel like this supplier can make the product?

Instead, we must let this question be our guide:

ASK: Does the supplier have his plant processes under control and the capability to make the product?

The first question elicits fuzzy answers. The answers to the second question can be objectively quantified, using the point values listed below as we record responses and gather evidence for the selection criteria:

Evaluation Criteria Point Value	
Points	**Statement**
5	The supplier's conditions are excellent (100% compliance).
4	The provisions meet 80% of the requirements.
3	The conditions' rank is average and functioning well (50% compliance).
2	The conditions are functioning at a 30% level.
1	The conditions are incomplete and functioning poorly (10% compliance).
0	No conditions are met.
N/A	Not applicable.

One further word about objectivity. There are two schools of thought about how to conduct surveys. One school says to send a survey out to suppliers and ask for their input, then to read the results and conduct on-site surveys. The second school of thought advocates going directly to the supplier first to conduct surveys. Which method you choose is subject to many variables, but we hold with the second school. We want to avoid a company responding in a positive way, then leaving us later to determine if the survey was completed correctly.

There is some material that can be obtained before conducting a survey. Information like annual financial reports, 10K's, and supplier quality manuals are acceptable pre-survey material since they are more objective. Other areas, however, need to be explored at the supplier's plant with workers and managers so we can make objective judgments based on the evidence.

Before conducting a survey, we should also be prepared to have the appropriate members of our team pose the right questions to the supplier's representatives. Know in advance who will talk to the supplier's Finance, Engineering, Manufacturing and Quality departments. The team is drawn from the people involved in developing the supplier selection criteria. Their questions should start broadly and progressively focus on an area of detail.

SUPPLIER SURVEY CHECKLIST

At the beginning of this chapter, we identified eight major areas of criteria used when surveying suppliers. Let's look at them in more detail and identify some of the questions we should ask suppliers for each area. At the end of this chapter, you will find another example of a supplier survey.

QUALITY MANAGEMENT

The key to the management of quality comes from the supplier's philosophy, objectives and organizational structure.

YES   NO   PTS.   EVALUATION

—   —   —   Quality philosophy is adequate and explained in operating policies and procedures.

—   —   —   People responsible for quality are technically competent.

—   —   —   Organizational structure defines quality responsibility and authority.

—   —   —   Top management is accessible to direct labor.

—   —   —   Quality manual is adequately documented and conforms with regulatory requirements.

—   —   —   Education and training program exists and is complete.

GOALS AND OBJECTIVES: To determine whether management is integrally involved in quality and whether responsibility and authority for quality extends to the operator level.

DESIGN INFORMATION

Design should not be an isolated department. The design of products and the processes to make them are a team effort.

YES	NO	PTS.	EVALUATION
—	—	—	Operators are given complete technical instructions for the manufacturing and inspection of the product.
—	—	—	Records reflect design changes and pertinent data.
—	—	—	Quality/manufacturing ensures that changes are implemented effectively.
—	—	—	Design information is available to all personnel.
—	—	—	Formal deviation and corrective action procedure is present and followed.

GOALS AND OBJECTIVES: To ensure that all current design information is accurate and timely and that procedures are in place to guarantee continued accuracy and timeliness.

PROCUREMENT

The customer's quality requirements should be the same as those of the manufacturer's suppliers.

<u>YES</u> <u>NO</u> <u>PTS.</u> <u>EVALUATION</u>

YES	NO	PTS.	EVALUATION
—	—	—	Sources are evaluated and monitored continuously.
—	—	—	Quality requirements are adequately specified.
—	—	—	Inspection procedures are specified and followed for all levels of the operation.
—	—	—	Inspection facilities and equipment are present and maintained by operators, quality, etc.
—	—	—	Certified suppliers are used instead of inspection.
—	—	—	Corrective action procedures are present and used.

GOALS AND OBJECTIVES: To verify that procurement procedures are in place which guarantee consistent quality, delivery and quantity.

MATERIAL CONTROL

The right material must not only be procured and verified, but
identified and controlled to assure that it gets to the right place
at the right time.

YES   NO   PTS.   EVALUATION

___   ___   ___   Procedures for storage,
                     release and movement of
                     material have high degree
                     of accuracy.

___   ___   ___   Inventory is identified and
                     controlled. Either lot
                     control or traceability is in
                     existence.

___   ___   ___   Work-In-Process material is
                     identified and controlled.

___   ___   ___   Access to stored material
                     is controlled.

___   ___   ___   Procedures covering de-
                     terioration, corrosion and
                     hazardous waste materials
                     are followed.

GOALS AND OBJECTIVES: To seek the control of material
flow from the time it reaches the receiving dock to the time it is
shipped.

MANUFACTURING CONTROL

Quality characteristics can best be verified during the production process.

YES NO PTS. EVALUATION

— — — Process capabilities are established and maintained by operators and engineering.

— — — In-process inspection is conducted by the operator.

— — — In-process inspection promotes effective corrective action.

— — — Procedures for equipment and facility maintenance programs are present.

— — — Statistical Process Control is employed.

GOALS AND OBJECTIVES: To institute procedures which guarantee that quality control is done in-process.

FINAL INSPECTION

Final inspection should be gradually phased out to be replaced by process control.

YES   NO   PTS.   EVALUATION

—   —   —   Specifications are properly used in determining acceptability of material.

—   —   —   Certifications and in-process inspection records are used in final acceptance decisions.

—   —   —   Inspection procedures are complete and followed.

—   —   —   Inspection facilities and equipment are capable and under control.

—   —   —   Inspection results are used in corrective action procedures.

—   —   —   Cause and effect solutions to problems exist.

GOALS AND OBJECTIVES: To determine how dependent a company is on final inspection and what plans they have to move toward process control.

CALIBRATION

Inaccurate calibration of fixtures and equipment can result in either the rejection of good material or the acceptance of defective material.

<u>YES</u> <u>NO</u> <u>PTS.</u> <u>EVALUATION</u>

—   —   —   Internal standards conform to and are checked against national standards.

—   —   —   Inspections and calibrations are scheduled frequently enough to ensure equipment is never out of calibration.

—   —   —   Calibration facilities and equipment are capable.

—   —   —   External calibration sources are utilized.

GOALS AND OBJECTIVES: To maintain calibration standards which are consistent and conform to national or industry standards.

Supplier Certification

QUALITY INFORMATION

Unused or unusable data is evidence of poor management.

YES	NO	PTS.	EVALUATION
—	—	—	Records of inspections and tests are maintained in order to review data.
—	—	—	Data in the quality control operation is used to increase or decrease the amount of inspection.
—	—	—	A closed-loop, product quality system is evident in a corrective action process.
—	—	—	A document of certification verifying product quality is given to customers.
—	—	—	Quality results and trends are reported to management.
—	—	—	Cost of quality data exist.

GOALS AND OBJECTIVES: To ensure that quality data is used to improve the operations.

POST-SURVEY ACTIVITY

Once a survey has been conducted and evaluated, the next job is to write a final report which recommends whether or not a supplier is capable of being certified. A copy of this final report should certainly be sent to the supplier, whatever the recommendation. We have seen many instances of suppliers who have taken areas of weakness and turned them into positive programs of improvement. Many of these suppliers have eventually gone on to become certified. In a certain sense, the final report is free consulting. Companies that want to improve their performance will use it to their advantage.

As for the recommendation, there are three categories. Each requires a different set of post-survey activities.

1. <u>NOT RECOMMENDED</u>:

The supplier, in this case, has no evidence or documentation of a control system; major defects in its control system; or, cannot demonstrate an acceptable process. The deficiency in the control system and/or process will require in excess of 60 days to correct.

A "Vendor Corrective Action" report will be issued requesting correction of these discrepancies. Upon receipt of satisfactory answers, a re-survey will be required. At that time, the supplier may be moved to a conditional status.

2. <u>CONDITIONALLY RECOMMENDED TO THE AVL LIST</u>:

The supplier has inadequacies in its control system documentation, but the process or processes appear to be working satisfactorily. A "Vendor Corrective Action" report will be issued requesting the supplier to correct the discrepancies. If the discrepancies are not corrected within 60 days, the rating will be changed to "Not Recommended."

For suppliers in this category, we should sign a conditional agreement with the supplier like the one below:

CONDITIONAL AGREEMENT

THE DISCREPANCY AND/OR DEFICIENCIES DESCRIBED IN THIS REPORT ARE VERIFIED AND WILL BE CORRECTED BY:

_____   _____

DATE   COMPANY NAME

VENDOR STATUS WILL BE UPGRADED TO "RECOMMENDED" WHEN PURCHASING RECEIVES WRITTEN EVIDENCE OF THE PROMISED CORRECTIVE ACTION ON OR BEFORE THE AGREED DATE AND DETERMINES THAT IT IS ADEQUATE.

_____   _____

DATE   SUPPLIER SIGNATURE

                        _____

                        TITLE

3. <u>RECOMMENDED TO THE QVL LIST:</u>

The supplier has adequate document evidence of compliance to the stated control system and the demonstrated process appears to be working satisfactorily. Within this category are suppliers who are ready and willing to undergo the certification process. The next step, then, is to develop a procurement quality agreement.

APPENDIX

SUPPLIER CERTIFICATION PROGRAM

AUDIT FORM

SECTION 1   **MANAGEMENT**

SECTION 2   **PREVENTIVE MAINTENANCE**

SECTION 3   **MATERIALS MANAGEMENT**

SECTION 4   **CORRECTIVE ACTION SYSTEM**

SECTION 5   **QUALITY CONTROL**

SECTION 6   **RECORD ACCURACY/CONTROL**

SECTION 7   **MANUFACTURING OPERATION**

SECTION 8   **PROCESS CONTROL**

SECTION 9   **PACKAGING AND SHIPPING**

SECTION 1   MANAGEMENT

SCORE   ASSESSMENT

_____   **Are performance measurements regularly reported to management?**

_____   **Does management use quality data to make improvements?**

_____   **Does management have an effective and comprehensive long-term business plan?**

_____   **Is there an adequate and continuous training and education program?**

_____   **What is the financial situation of the company? (Obtain a copy of annual report.)**

_____   **Is management receptive to innovation both from its own employees and from customers?**

_____   **How well does the supplier manage its own suppliers and subcontractors?**

SECTION 2   PREVENTIVE MAINTENANCE

SCORE   **ASSESSMENT**

_____   Is the building and facilities well maintained and free from outside elements?

_____   Are safety and housekeeping audits scheduled on a regular basis?

_____   Are there written procedures for reporting deviations from preventive maintenance standards?

_____   Has the supplier ever been cited by a governmental regulatory agency for violations?

_____   Is there adequate space for the orderly placement of hazardous material?

_____   What is the general condition of storage material such as pallets, etc.?

_____   Is the lighting sufficient?

SECTION 3   MATERIALS MANAGEMENT

<u>SCORE</u>   <u>ASSESSMENT</u>

_____   **Does the supplier have a Supplier Certification program in place for its suppliers?**

_____   **Is rework submitted for reinspection?**

_____   **Do records reflect accurate quantities and delivery dates?**

_____   **Does a manual exist for receiving material? How effectively is it followed?**

_____   **Do the supplier's testing procedures match the customer's?**

_____   **Are the supplier's test results monitored?**

_____   **Are the testing results and procedures well documented?**

_____   **Are test procedures reviewed and audited on a periodic basis?**

_____   **Are test results control-charted?**

SECTION 4   CORRECTIVE ACTION SYSTEM

SCORE   ASSESSMENT

_____   Is non-conforming material identified as such by stickers or some other form of identification to separate it from approved material?

_____   How effective is the system which identifies and processes ship-ments approved, rejected or awaiting inspection?

_____   Does the corrective action system for non-conforming product prevent and control recurring defects?

_____   Are there written procedures for returning non-conforming material to the supplier?

_____   Are customers notified of potential non-conforming material? How soon?

_____   Are written records maintained so as to identify recurring defects?

SECTION 5   QUALITY CONTROL

SCORE   ASSESSMENT

_____   Is a training and education
program in place for all Quality
Control personnel?

_____   Is quality data used in conjunction
with the certification requirements
of the customer?

_____   Are Quality Control manuals used
throughout the plant?

_____   Can Quality Control stop shipment
of finished product if necessary?

_____   Are statistical controls used for
in-process inspection?

_____   Are there written quality control
instructions for line inspectors?

_____   Is a routine followed for equipment start-up, changeovers,
adjustments to ensure that the
machine will make it right the
first time?

_____   Are inspection records on file?

SECTION 6 RECORD ACCURACY/CONTROL

<u>SCORE</u>   <u>ASSESSMENT</u>

_____   Is there a back-up record system
                in place?

_____   Are obsolete drawings and
                specifications removed from use?

_____   Is there a documented system in
                place for communicating changes
                made to records?

_____   Are there controls over who can
                make revisions to work instruc-
                tions, blueprints, etc.?

_____   Are current documents free of
                handwritten and unofficial
                changes?

_____   Are inspection reports regularly
                reviewed by qualified personnel?

_____   Does the Quality Control group
                have the most recent copies of
                specifications? Engineering?

_____   Is there a list of documents to
                be controlled?

SECTION 7   MANUFACTURING OPERATION

<u>SCORE</u>   <u>ASSESSMENT</u>

_____   **Are manufactured lots traceable throughout the process?**

_____   **How is the maximum tool life determined by the supplier?**

_____   **Does the process sheet accurately show the correct machine or work center?**

_____   **Is there a system for periodic preventive maintenance on manufacturing equipment?**

_____   **Do records show calibration and traceability which reflects national standards?**

_____   **Is the calibration procedure conducted under favorable environmental conditions?**

_____   **Are manufacturing equipment and tools, including personal equipment, calibrated according to a formal procedure?**

SECTION 8   PROCESS CONTROL

SCORE   ASSESSMENT

_____   **Is a formal training and education program in place for personnel directly involved in the manufacture and control of material?**

_____   **Is cross-training practiced for all manufacturing personnel?**

_____   **Is Statistical Process Control being used?**

_____   **Do critical points in the process have process controls set up?**

_____   **Is process control information used to identify the causes of problems?**

_____   **Are personnel trained in problem-solving techniques?**

_____   **Does the process control system initiate a corrective action when processes fall out of limits?**

_____   **Is there a set-up reduction program present in the plant?**

SECTION 9 PACKAGING AND SHIPPING

SCORE ASSESSMENT

_____ Is a Certificate of Compliance to Specifications and test results included with the shipment? Is it signed by an authorized person?

_____ Are there written procedures for what enclosures to include with each shipment?

_____ How are packing specifications maintained?

_____ Is standard packaging used?

_____ Is Bar Coding used in the process?

_____ Are traffic and routing sheets displayed for all personnel to see?

_____ How is delivery time measured? What percentage of deliveries are on time?

_____ Is hazardous material handled and shipped in a safe manner?

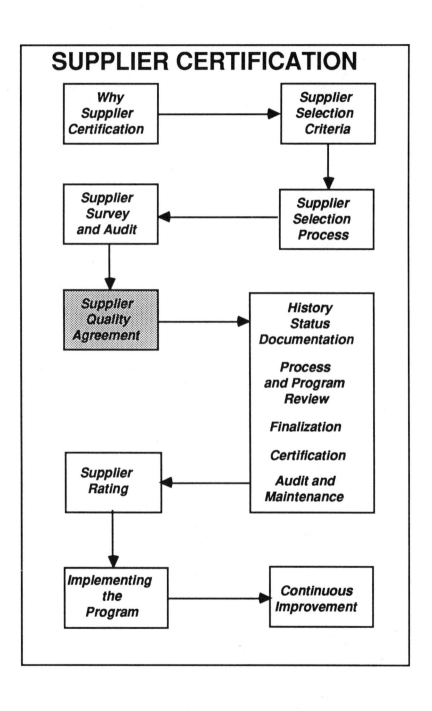

SUPPLIER CERTIFICATION

Why Supplier Certification → **Supplier Selection Criteria**

Supplier Survey and Audit ← **Supplier Selection Process**

Supplier Quality Agreement →

History
Status
Documentation

Process
and Program
Review

Finalization

Certification

Audit and
Maintenance

Supplier Rating ←

Implementing the Program → **Continuous Improvement**

TOTAL QUALITY CONTROL

Basis for a Procurement Quality Agreement

5

The Procurement Quality Agreement spells out the responsibilities of both the manufacturer and the supplier in the certification process. It is not a purchase order. It works in conjunction with purchasing agreements, blanket orders or system contracts. It is a mutually developed document which simply provides that the supplier delivers parts which conform to requirements 100% of the time. Its purpose is to state responsibilities before the product is made.

Before we discuss some of the specific components of a quality agreement, let's first take time to preview the foundation of Total Quality Control. The purpose of the quality document is to bring a supplier's manufacturing process under control in order to negate the necessity of any form of inspection.

TOTAL QUALITY CONTROL (TQC)

Supplier Certification rests on the bedrock of quality. This is something that the Japanese first learned in the 1950s when Deming was invited to present his quality philosophy. Up to that time, Japanese companies had a reputation for producing low quality items. Then they realized that, in order to compete, they would need to start paying attention to quality. Deming showed the Japanese how to improve quality. Most importantly, the Japanese listened while their American counterparts seemed content to rest on their laurels. Not so ironically, the threat of competition is now driving American companies to embrace Total Quality Control for their survival.

As manufacturers, we need to commit ourselves to working with suppliers to ensure customer satisfaction through total conformance to quality requirements. At the same time, we should be developing suppliers who are dedicated to the continuous improvement of quality. In essence, a Supplier Certification program requires:

KEY QUALITY REQUIREMENTS

1. Reliability over a period of time, meaning consistent deliveries, product and conformance to customer requirements.

2. Burden of quality is on the supplier's control of its process, not on inspection techniques.

BASIC PRINCIPLES OF QUALITY

These rules form the operating philosophy for improving supplier quality through a certification program. This philosophy requires basic principles which will govern both short-term and long-term activities. These principles are:

• *A control process by which to check, measure and report.*

Statistical Process Control (SPC)
Statistical Manufacturing Control (SMC)
Acceptable Quality Level (A Quick Look) (AQL)

The determination of what is to be measured is equally as important as the method or technique used. SPC and SMC are quality tools used by various industries, mathematical techniques which determine where a process is in relation to established upper and lower control limits.

Although you may use AQL, we don't view it as the primary measuring tool for the long run. AQL is an evolutionary step we will go through before we move on to SPC. We recommend using AQL as a problem-solving technique to determine the differences between causes and effects, rather than as a way to segregate bad from good parts as we do today.

• *A program that is visible to all levels of operation.*

The results of a quality program should be visible to all

levels of personnel. This information must be displayed, clearly defining the goals we are trying to achieve and the measurements we use. As quality levels improve, the movement upward on a chart is an effective impetus to further improvement. Some companies are hesitant to display graphs or charts on the walls of their factories because customers often tour their plants. One company told the receptionist to alert the factory floor whenever an inspector or customer would make a visit. Factory personnel then had 15 minutes to take the charts down.

We believe this is wrong for two reasons. First, it sends the wrong message to the workers on the floor that the company has something to hide. Second, whether it is an inspector or a customer, most people are understanding and supportive of a company which is trying to improve its quality. Honesty, therefore, is not only the morally right thing to do, but it is also the economically right thing to do. Don't display charts one week and fail to post progress on them. This only provides a mixed message to employees who will begin to question your company's commitment to excellence.

• *Compliance of material requirements and specifications.*

This principle can be easily understood. A company should have in place whatever materials, fixtures, tools and equipment that are required to perform the job within specifications.

• *The support of management.*

>Management support is the oil which keeps the machinery of quality improvement functioning smoothly. Its presence is critical to the morale and engagement of all levels of the organization. If the different levels of the company don't feel that management is involved and committed, then their support and contributions will be limited.

• *A new mind-set and culture.*

>This principle fosters a culture which accepts new projects and changes. It assumes that there are no sacred cows in a company and that all operations and procedures are open to scrutiny and improvement. Furthermore, a zero-defect mentality must permeate all levels of a company. There must be established and clear lines of authority. Only when operators are given the authority and responsibility for quality will it have an effect on improvements. If that requires stopping the production line to fix the true causes of a problem, then *production lines must be stopped.*

POINTS OF THE AGREEMENT

ZERO-DEFECT PROGRAMS

The principles of a zero-defect program support the philosophy of Total Quality Control:

>• **Conformance** — meeting all customer requirements.

- **Process** — delivering only what you need.
- **Tracking** — knowing the results and how they compare to the goal.
- **Measurement** — being able to measure the results of the program.
- **Corrective action** — fixing the problem.

CONFORMANCE TO REQUIREMENTS

Much is said about conformance to requirements, but most of it assumes that conformance is exclusively a management problem. We view conformance more broadly. What other questions are implicit in the accepted definition that conformance is a product meeting the requirements set forth by the specifications?

- Does it meet the customer needs?
- Does it meet the engineering specifications?
- Does it meet the manufacturing process requirements?
- Does the product meet the test requirements?

We believe that products should meet their customer requirements. The problem with American manufacturers is that they are not inclined to determine what is needed or wanted by their customers. A good example is custom corrugated cartons. We know of a situation in which a company using custom cartons could fit its product into standard cartons simply by adjusting one dimension. They had difficulty changing the dimension because it wasn't in the specifications and had to be sent to Engineering Change Control. They then had to see whether the change made any difference to their customers. In many cases, the change made no difference and they were able to lower the total cost.

It pays to make it right the first time, but this requires close communication and documentation of the actions between Engineering and Manufacturing. Supplier Certification addresses this by demanding:

- A flexible system in which every company level, not just management, is responsible for quality.

- Accurate and timely maintenance of route sheets, processes and Bills of Material.

- Accurate and timely maintenance of effectivity dates.

- A system of no variances to specifications.

QUALITY AT THE SOURCE

Employees should be held accountable for performing their job correctly. For example, a client manufacturing a product noticed that cartons coming down the production line were being filled with various components. At the end of the line, an inspector would open the box to make sure everything was inside and packed carefully. This is inspection after the fact. The company established a system so that each worker would be held accountable for making sure the components from the previous person were there to begin with. This is quality at the source.

The source of quality must originate at both the supplier's and company's production level and then work its way to the customers. Strange as it may sound, this is similar to what the People's Republic of China did when it set out to modernize its economic system. Unlike the Soviets, who are attempting to revitalize from the top down, the Chinese began with small family farms. By starting at the lowest economic level, their economic revitalization has proven far more successful than the Soviets' much more bureaucratic method.

Ground-level participation also boosts morale. People feel as though they are contributing to the production of quality materials. Thus, we should eventually eliminate sampling techniques such as AQL (MIL STD 105D). Implementing quality at the source with the involvement of workers is the objective. A 2% AQL is not good enough in today's competitive environment. One only needs to look at the chart below to see the consequences of operating at this level:

<u>WHAT TO EXPECT FROM A 2% AQL</u>

- **At least 20,000 wrong drug prescriptions each year.**

- **More than 15,000 newborn babies accidentally dropped by doctors or nurses each year.**

- **Two short or long landings at O'Hare airport each day (also New York, Los Angeles, Atlanta, etc.)**

- **Nearly 500 incorrect surgical operations per week.**

When customers demand 100% quality and provide the testing, education and training, we can compete. By accepting two out of 100 parts as bad, we have established a policy of self-destruction. In fact, the first pass yield is only 17% for a product comprised of 100 parts which are subject to a 2% AQL. To go beyond a 2% AQL and reach 100% accuracy 100% of the time means paying attention to three major areas:

> **Operator** — Internal and external suppliers must be trained in quality techniques like Statistical Process Control (SPC). A quality manual must be used and not sit on a manager's shelf. Operators should know exactly what quality means and its effect on the operation.

> **Machine** — Operators must be capable of demonstrating how SPC is conducted on a machine. There must be documented evidence that the machine is capable of performing within the established control limits 100% of the time.

> **Process** — There must be documented evidence that the entire process is under control. SPC provides a tool for measuring process variables.

These three areas lay the groundwork for one of the cornerstones of Supplier Certification — Statistical Process Control (SPC).

STATISTICAL PROCESS CONTROL

We can no longer conduct business in an environment which

accepts previous high levels of scrap, rework, waste and delays. Establishing process control is the new level of excellence. Statistical Process Control is an effective method of evaluating a process to identify both desirable and undesirable changes. Armand V. Feigenbaum's *TOTAL QUALITY CONTROL* contains an excellent discussion of statistical methods. The result of Statistical Process Control is to produce a product which conforms to requirements while the product is in process.

STATISTICAL

Statistical means using numbers and data which are recorded from observations. Some types of data collection or measuring are:

- Run charts.
- Check sheets.
- Graphs.
- Histograms.
- Pareto charts.

PROCESS

SPC can also measure the effectiveness of a *process* by using statistical data to determine what is the capability of the machine or its operational activities (machines, people and material):

- Sampling.
- Data collection.
- Stratification.
- Normal frequency distribution.
- Standard deviation.
- Control charts.

CONTROL

Control makes the process behave the way we want it to.

Employees trained in SPC use process control charts while charting a process in order to keep it under control. Operators need to learn only four rules in order to chart processes. First, they must know what is a correct part and why. Second, they must have ways of determining if a part is right. Third, they must have the means to monitor a change over time in order to prevent defects. Fourth, they must have instructions on how to adjust or change the process before defects occur.

Now you are ready to let operators benefit from the training by keeping statistical records of their machine's operation. These will take the form of a control chart. But, before operators at a supplier start using control charts, they must establish that the process is capable. We need to set some precontrol rules for a simple and effective method of allowing them to control the process. Given sample sizes of five parts for set-ups and five consecutive parts at regular intervals, or continuous during run time, the precontrol rules say:

SET-UP:

OK to run when six readings are inside the target area. The target is defined as the area within an upper and lower control limit. This requirement is for the set-up portion only.

RUNNING:

1. If results are inside target area, continue to run.

2. As results tend toward control limits, operator may continue to run until one falls outside of control limits.

3. No parts are allowed to go beyond the specification limits and remain with good parts.

Results are tabulated on a control chart like the one depicted here for a machined steel shaft whose limits are plus or minus .003 inches. Tests are conducted to determine where the upper and lower control limits are placed in order to ensure with greater than 99.73% accuracy that only acceptable parts are produced.

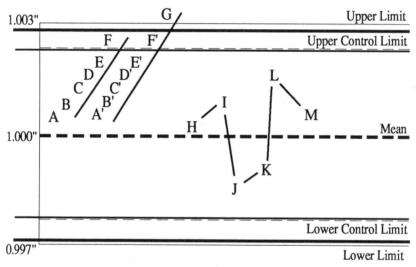

PROCESS CONTROL CHART

The operator of this particular machine which makes the shafts would then begin to make parts as soon as six consecutive parts fall within the area between UCL and LCL. This would complete the set-up. Now the operator would begin the run. The first part (A) measures slightly more than 1 inch. B through E gradually deviate further from the mean, but in a predictable pattern. In this case, it would probably indicate that the cutting tool was wearing. Repeated use allows the part to grow as the tool wears down. Predictably, the sixth part (F) falls beyond the upper control limit. It is still, however, within specification limits. Therefore, the part is not rejected, but the process is adjusted.

What happens when the operator measures a part that falls at G? The operator then physically separates the part from other produced pieces and *STOPS* the process. She calls over her supervisor or consults a troubleshooting guide to see why the process went wrong. She should not make another part until the problem is corrected. She does not treat the symptom and hope for the best.

Finally, what does it mean when an operator charts measurements which appear like H through L? They are all in the control limits, all perfectly acceptable. But, they do not depict a predictable pattern. Such a chart indicates that the process may be out of control. Here, too, the operator stops her run and finds out why the machine is performing erratically.

As we have said before, JIT and TQC require that we provide the operator with responsibility and authority. These charts clearly show how this works in real-world situations. Each operator is responsible for charting his or her own machine's process and has the authority to stop the machine when parts fall out of predictable patterns or beyond acceptable limits.

If your supplier has SPC in place, you can be assured of two things

— higher quality parts and, most importantly, a process which will continue to produce zero-defect parts. That is why SPC at the supplier's plant is an important part of Supplier Certification.

However, it doesn't stop here. There must be on-going education and a program to promote quality. Quality must be a way of life or, as Ford Motor Company's motto says, "Quality is Job 1." A poorly designed product fights an uphill battle, maybe even a losing battle, against quality. If you are going to make it right the first time, you must design it right the first time.

QUALITY PROBLEM-SOLVING — CAUSE AND EFFECT DIAGRAMS

The major problem that manufacturers encounter when using statistical methods is an inability to define the process and the characteristics to be studied. We don't know how to use statistical reporting to find the real causes of problems. This is because the responsibility for problem-solving is poorly defined by management. Most control systems are inadequate or misunderstood and the approaches to problem-solving are unstructured.

You may also be guilty of attacking the whole problem instead of sizing up the problem and then attacking its parts. We also tend to treat symptoms instead of curing causes. Management often focuses on short-term solutions which miss treating the real cause of a problem.

One effective problem-identification technique is the cause and effect (fishbone) diagram as shown on the next page. The intent is to identify a problem and its possible causes and then to note which causes are being worked on and which are done.

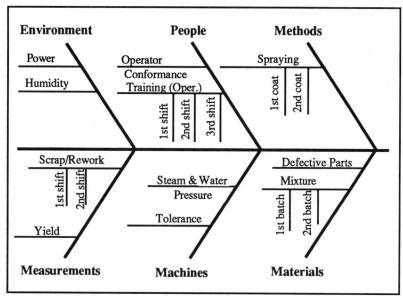

Cause Enumeration Fishbone

In our example, you can undoubtedly see that one problem may have causes in a number of areas. For example, is "inaccurate measurement" a machine problem, a measurement problem or a manpower problem? It is not so important where you place the problem on the fishbone as it is to identify the problem and causes. If you spend too much time deciding what goes where, you could contract the dreaded disease of "paralysis through analysis." We warn you not to study a plan to death. Problem-solving is more than identification; it is action.

CORRECTION STEPS FOR DEVIATION

Once the problem is identified, then we are ready to work with the supplier to correct the deviation using these steps:

<u>**CORRECTION STEPS FOR DEVIATIONS**</u>

• **Develop specific goals and have the right tools.**

• **Identify exactly what is out of control.**
    Accumulate data (reports)
    Summarize data on one sheet of paper
    Chart data so it is understandable to the
        layperson and the operator

• **Discuss a solution.**
    Break diagnosis into manageable units
    Analyze data
    Define problem and brainstorm

• **Initiate action.**
    Develop a plan for new standards
    Utilize feedback
    Monitor
    Establish control so action remains
        consistent with overall process and
        timely completion (target date)

THE COST OF QUALITY

Continuous improvement of quality not only moves you toward zero-defect products, but increases savings as well. The cost of quality divides into three classifications — Prevention Costs, Appraisal Costs and Failure Costs.

Prevention Costs	Base Line Formula	Month Actual Dollars	YTD Actual Dollars
Design reviews			
Qualification testing			
Parts qualification			
Supplier qualification			
Supplier quality seminars			
Specification reviews			
Process control studies			
Tool control			
Eng. quality training			
Operational training			
Quality orientation			
Acceptance planning			
Zero-defect pgms.			
Statistical training			
Quality audits			
Drawings reviews			
Preventive maint.			
Automation			

A Base Line Formula is an assigned dollar value given to each area in order to ensure that a point in time is documented. It is similar to a benchmark.

Appraisal Costs	Base Line Formula	Month Actual Dollars	YTD Actual Dollars
Prototype inspection			
Acceptance testing			
Supplier qualification			
Product inspection			
Marketing service survey			
Incoming inspection			
Pkg. inspection			
Inventory audit			
Matl. review board			
Process control tests			
Production spec.			
Conformance testing			

The last two classifications, appraisal and failure, are typical of costs incurred by manufacturers using traditional quality methods. They are the costs associated with products which do not conform to requirements. Prevention costs, on the other hand, are more in keeping with TQC. Not surprisingly, spending more on

Failure Costs	Base Line Formula	Month Actual Dollars	YTD Actual Dollars
Scrap			
Rework			
Warranty			
Product liability			
Corrective action			
Service			
Purch. change orders			
Eng. change orders			
Redesign			
Customer relations			

prevention and less on failure and appraisal costs will increase savings as the toaster chart (published in an article which we wrote for *Production and Inventory Management Review*) on the next page shows.

The prevention cost chart can be used for budgeting purposes. It will clearly show the dollars required in this area and certainly put pressure on management to commit itself to spending those dollars.

The cost of quality is usually greatly underestimated by most

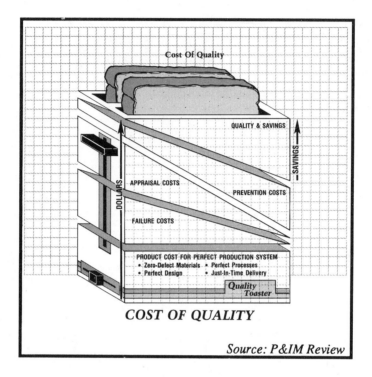

COST OF QUALITY

Source: P&IM Review

companies. The Quality Cost chart shows that when a company has a low level of quality understanding, actual costs increase dramatically. As the company grows more mature, the more realistic reported costs will become.

Prevention and Supplier Certification become a way of life when the reported cost of quality equals the actual cost. At this level, we have control over the process. This is also the level at which we want suppliers to be. The quality agreement spells out the goals and the intervening steps which suppliers agree to take in order to become certified. Certification can be accomplished easily and quickly with the proper support.

Quality Cost as % of sales or operations			
Level	**Reported**	**Actual**	**% Accurate**
1 Hidden Inspector	Unknown	Unknown	0
2 Firefighter	3	10	33
3 Involved Managers	8	12	50
4 Effective Officers	6.5	8	81
5 TQC: a Way of Life	2.5	2.5	100

DUTIES OF THE SUPPLIER QUALITY ENGINEER (SQE)

The position of Supplier Quality Engineer has several critical duties. The most important is establishing a line of communication between the supplier and the customer. The SQE acts as an interface between the customer and the supplier's departments.

At the start of a quality program, both sides must sit down and clearly define what is expected in the demonstrated process areas. The first area is establishing performance goals. Here, we should make clear exactly what we want from the supplier in terms of conformance to requirements and in the establishment of correct specifications. The next area is establishing the existence of procedures and process documents. The goal is to receive components at our plants which require no inspection. The third area is the implementation of control procedures. This includes defining procedures and how to use them in the supplier's organization. The fourth area is defining what goals we want the supplier to achieve. The most important goal is to continuously work toward improving the product and total cost. The last area is procedure improvements. Here, we want to establish the procedures which are needed to improve the overall process.

Prior to a Supplier Certification program, most of these activities were covered by inspection. This meant inspection of the end result of a process and little communication between the supplier and the manufacturer. This is also true of First Article inspection. All too often this means the inspection of the best samples culled from a production run. This is not a true indication of the quality of a part. The SQE must be an integrated part of the process that assists in improving the product. Let's review some of the SQE's duties:

DUTIES OF THE SUPPLIER
QUALITY ENGINEER

• **Audit product and process**

• **Perform dimensional/functional tests**

• **Maintain qualification/shipping records**

• **Communicate with customers/suppliers**

• **Verify completeness of specifications**

• **Guarantee accountability**

THE CONTENTS
OF A SUPPLIER QUALITY AGREEMENT

The agreement's purpose is to map out how the customer and the supplier will integrate all of the issues discussed in this chapter. As explained earlier, it will contain a statement of purpose and scope and set objectives:

TERMS AND CONDITIONS

• Sets quantity levels for raw material and Work-In-Process inventories which reflect flexible production schedules.

• Defines quality level as zero-defects.

• Controls price fluctuations and conditions for cost/price changes.

• Establishes delivery schedules and windows as well as shipping terms and packaging specifications.

• Defines terms of payment.

• Establishes responsibilities for corrective action in the event of non-conformance.

In order to have a true partnership, each side must be committed to meeting certain responsibilities. This is the core of any successful agreement. Neither side should feel as though they are being taken advantage of. The following chart illustrates some of the responsibilities of a quality partner:

RESPONSIBILITIES OF A QUALITY PARTNERSHIP

Manufacturer	Supplier
1. Process-achievable specifications	Evaluate process capability to meet customer specifications
2. Clear standards	Evaluate standards/methods
3. Clear line of communication	Clear line of communication
4. Notification of organizational changes	Notification of organizational changes
5. Discussion of potential changes in requirements	Discussion of potential changes in requirements
6. Assist supplier in solving quality, production problems	Notify customer of quality, production problems and capacity
7. Provide timely feedback and corrective action	Provide timely feedback and corrective action

8. Provide audit schedule   Notify customer of sourcing or process changes

9. Share audit results   Close feedback loop

10. Resolve supplier questions   Inform customer of new processes and/or materials

11. Commit to continuous improvement program   Commit to continuous improvement program

All is now set for the Supplier Certification process. We can't emphasize enough the necessity of building a solid foundation before you begin to qualify a supplier's process and components. An Olympic diver, for example, may make his sport look so graceful as to appear effortless. But he spends many long hours practicing the dive, exercising to get into peak shape and consulting with his coach on the finer points of technique. Great divers and great dives don't just happen. They are earned by long hours of commitment and dedication. It is just this type of mind-set that these beginning chapters have attempted to establish. They are lessons which demand much practice before they became part of a total quality mentality, but the rewards will be great. We, too, can make the plunge into the Phases of Certification appear as graceful as the most complicated dive.

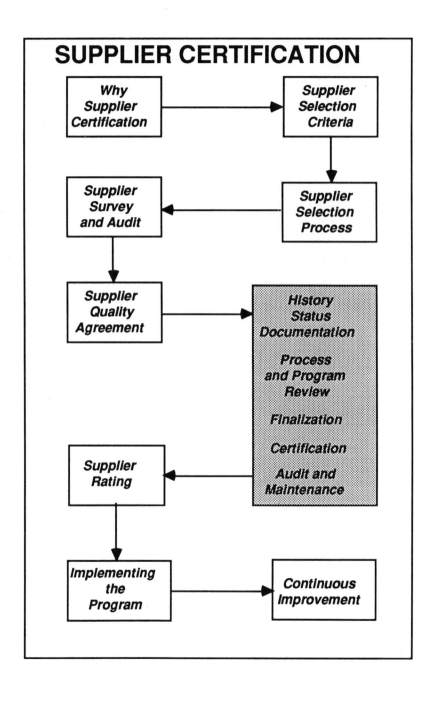

SUPPLIER CERTIFICATION

| Why Supplier Certification | → | Supplier Selection Criteria |

Supplier Survey and Audit ← **Supplier Selection Process**

Supplier Quality Agreement →

History
Status
Documentation

Process
and Program
Review

Finalization

Certification

Audit and
Maintenance

Supplier Rating ←

Implementing the Program → **Continuous Improvement**

PHASES OF CERTIFICATION

6

Quality at the source and shipping parts that conform to requirements and require no inspection are the primary objectives of Supplier Certification. We can achieve this by entering into a partnership with a supplier which is based on trust and cooperation. Establishing that partnership is a five-phase program. It entails gathering facts about a supplier, designing quality improvement processes, putting them into practice, and then auditing and maintaining the process based on results which are continuously gathered and jointly interpreted.

In this program, we can think of ourselves as medical researchers who take a patient and not only find a cure, but find the means for the patient's continued well-being. The five phases of Supplier

Certification are similar to the compilation of a medical history, the implementation of a nourishing diet and a schedule of exercise, and the institution of regular check-ups. The goal is to develop a relationship in which a healthy supplier will act according to the regimen of TQC and JIT.

PHASE ONE: History, Status, Documentation

In the first phase, we must determine if each supplier that was qualified earlier is in shape to work in a symbiotic relationship. To determine this, we assess the present health of quality, processes and controls. There are a number of areas to probe for each supplier and part number to be certified:

First Article Inspection Status

The first question we want answered is whether or not a first article inspection was performed on the part. A first article inspection requires that a production component be checked for each attribute and then determine if all standards and specifications have been met. We want to be sure that a sample or culled-out component is *not* sent for review. In many instances, an outside, independent service can be used to conduct the inspection.

If a first article inspection was performed, we want to be sure that its results measure up to requirements. In other words, does a part taken from the production line today match the original first article? Often, first articles do not accurately reflect production parts. For this reason, we may elect to perform a first article inspection at a later point in the process, depending on the criticality of the part number or production lot.

Incoming Quality Control History (IQC) and Line Fallout

Companies usually have compiled considerable information in this area. The problem is that the data is rarely organized. Our first step is to gather all available information so we can determine the major areas in which rejects occur. Equally important is determining whether parts are rejected for the same reason every time despite notices of previous corrective action notification to correct the problem. The supplier's responsibility is to inform us about line rejects they experience on each component. What you will most likely find is that much of the available data is marked *DW* ("Don't Work") without real cause being established. The major objective is to gain an understanding of all the available quality data and present this data in an orderly fashion to the supplier. The supplier's role is to provide us with the data needed for correlation. Quality problems must help us determine cause and effect on the production line. By reviewing the percentage of reject types, we can begin to isolate where the disease is located and what courses of action are required.

Part Documentation Review and Update

In this step, we ensure that all specifications, blueprints or drawings we send to the supplier are accurate and understood. There are few things more annoying and eventually detrimental than incorrect specifications from which the supplier must then build.

While Peter Grieco was working at Digital Equipment Corporation (DEC), he ran across a good example of how to solve a problem in part documentation. A supplier was having difficulties building a part to specifications. For a while, the problem was assumed to be the supplier's, until Pete asked the supplier to visit the plant with his copies of DEC's blueprints for the part. The supplier came in and spread several sets of blueprints on the table. "Which set do you want me to follow?" the supplier asked. "The one without the red marks," Peter replied. "They all have red marks depending on which engineer visited my plant," was the supplier's reply. It soon became apparent that the problem was not solely the supplier's.

Over 50% of the time, when comparing your prints or specifications with a supplier's, you will find the problem is yours. Numerous purchasing functions do not even include a current print with each purchase order. It is no wonder, then, that a supplier doesn't know which specification is correct.

Packaging Specification/Method of Shipment

With each supplier, we must identify the type of packaging required for each line item as well as the standard number of parts per unit. Standard packaging speeds delivery and greatly increases data accuracy. The classic example is a carton of eggs. We don't count the eggs to see if there is a dozen; we simply look for empty spaces. In addition to packaging, we must determine the best inbound routing and shipment method for each part.

Status of Production Tooling

Every tool has a production life expectancy. Each tool is also designed for a specific job. Most companies, however, have no idea of how many parts were produced off of a certain tool. Nor do they hesitate to use a prototype tool for a production job. But this data is required to ensure control over the process. Worn tools do not make quality parts. It is far better to replace an old tool before it reaches the end of its production life, than it is to push the tool beyond its capability.

Since this data is often hard to find, or nonexistent, we can estimate the status of production tooling by asking the supplier for tool purchase orders. From this data, we can determine how many tools were bought and when and then we can estimate how many parts can be produced off of a tool. We must remember that hard and accurate data is not always available, but that intelligent estimates will initially suffice.

Status of Inspection Tooling and Gauges

This area is similar to the above in that we need to know how often and when inspection tools are calibrated. We also need to determine whether the present inspection tools are tied into the process. In other words, do they test the part in process or do they inspect after the fact? Remember: a tool must never be totally out of calibration before it is adjusted back into specification. A control chart may be applicable here. Lastly, we must survey the existing inspection tools to see whether they are adequate for the job and whether the supplier may need duplicate tooling or more advanced fixtures.

Delivery Performance

Here we look for the delivery performance of a part over a period of time to find out if the supplier delivers on time. If a delivery window has been established with a +/- tolerance, then a review of adherence to the exact date is required to see what the actual performance is. On time delivery can only be measured against a committed delivery date with the supplier. If you ordered without lead time consideration, a supplier cannot be punished. Again, the idea is to establish a beginning point from which we can measure progress toward narrowing the delivery window.

Teamwork and Timing

Phase 1 is the longest phase because it lays the foundation for what follows. It is most often slowed down because of poor specifications, incomplete data and lack of support. There are ways to quicken the process even though Supplier Certification is not a short-term commitment. One way is to perform a risk analysis. Obviously, we can't take 13,000 months to conduct Phase 1 for 13,000 different part numbers. This will mean concentrating first on the major parts or commodity and taking a risk with suppliers who have demonstrated quality in the past. At a computer manufacturing plant, for example, they were able to certify 67% of their suppliers' part numbers in the first year. In the third year of the program, they were up to 80%.

The second way to hasten Phase 1 is to form a team of people from Purchasing, Engineering, Manufacturing and Quality Assurance. They are the minimum required to support this phase.

The other important member of the team is, of course, the supplier. The leader of the supplier's team should be the person with the most enthusiasm for and interest in the program. Often, we have found, it is also the busiest person, the one who gets things done. If your goal is quality at the lowest level of the organization, then the leader should *not* be the Quality Manager. He or she can be a consultant to the project or a catalyst on the team, but we believe that the leader should be someone who has the final responsibility for the product.

Teamwork also means numerous visits to the supplier's plant to review the supplier's manufacturing and quality process. Evaluation by a multi-disciplined team means that details will not be overlooked.

PHASE TWO: Supplier Program Review and Process Evaluation

Submit Phase 1 Findings to Supplier

The preliminary research done, it is now time to take your data and review it with the supplier. Concurrently, the supplier submits its data to you. This documentation consists of process and quality data either required or existing on a part number. The next step is to sit down at a table and review all the documentation and analyze all the data so as to establish an understanding of the performance of the part in the past.

Supplier Process Review

The first review step determines whether the supplier's process is under control and what areas need to brought under control. If you find that the process is not under control, you must then determine the steps required to achieve process control. At this point, you may determine that SPC should be employed.

Quality Survey

In this step, we go back to the supplier selection criteria we developed earlier and determine whether the supplier meets the minimum requirements we established. If he doesn't, then we look for ways to work with that supplier to improve its position or look for a new source.

Evaluation Memo

Once these surveys are completed, we will undoubtedly find problems and weak areas which need strengthening. Our next step is to document all differences of opinion in an Evaluation Memo. Both sides sign this agreement which summarizes all corrective actions and constructs a time frame for their completion. The memo also assigns the responsibility and authority for addressing each issue to one specific person. That person commits to a finish date and a start date as well. This ensures that the person does not wait until the last minute to complete the task.

Review of Supplier Responses

This step is a review of all the documentation until it is mutually agreed that the specifications can be met. By that, we mean that both parties agree that it is accurate and free of ambiguities.

Phase 2 takes time to complete. By the end of this time, the question arises of whether or not the supplier is committed and capable of making the part to specification each time. If the answer is "no," then we either keep negotiating over the documentation, change the specifications so that the supplier can meet them or find another supplier. Before you can proceed to Phase 3, an agreement must be reached on the specifications.

PHASE THREE: Finalization

In this phase, we have reached an agreement that the supplier can make parts that conform to our requirements. We must ensure that all the courses of corrective action delineated in the Evaluation Memo have been completed. We must then agree on how to handle testing and methods of inspection for the supplier's product in order to reach full certification.

Finalization is the most difficult phase of Supplier Certification. The team must determine the number of acceptable lots that will prove a supplier can consistently deliver zero-defect parts. Our task is to set a level of lots which must come into our factory with no defects before the supplier can be certified. One technique for implementing this phase is to use a number of approaches which gradually move us away from incoming inspection. For example, establish 20 lots of zero-defect parts as the criteria. For the first 10 lots, perform a standard sampling plan to determine if the supplier is making the part to print. The next 10 lots could then be skip lots; that is, every other lot gets reviewed.

The number of lots must be established with the supplier as well as the type of inspection. Full certification and the absence of incoming inspection depends upon the criticality of the part. The number of lots and the type of inspection will be determined by what it takes to satisfy our requirements. The first two phases are there to gain control over the supplier's process for making the part. If they have been done correctly, we can trust the supplier to make zero-defect parts that meet the requirements of the customer. Therefore, we can make the inspection criteria as tough or easy as we want, based on what we are buying and how critical that is to our own production processes. Supplier Certification does not get rid of all incoming inspection. We will always have reliability labs and failure testing. But, Supplier Certification can and will greatly decrease our reliance on incoming inspection. We must simply change our frame of mind from inspecting parts to verifying processes.

There are some companies that set a time period for inspection, rather than the number of lots. For example, they might say that if there are no rejects in six months, then the supplier will be certified. We have problems with this method. It is conceivable that a six-month supply of parts can all be from one lot. The supplier has produced and warehoused the entire amount. This tells us very little about how much control he has over the process since there is only documentation for one lot. We want to see that a supplier can consistently make zero-defect parts and deliver them to us in smaller lots at more frequent delivery dates. Remember that Just-In-Time is based on the flexibility that smaller lots and reduced set-up times provide to the manufacturer.

Phase 3 completion, as outlined above, depends on the frequency of deliveries. With more frequent deliveries, more lots can be inspected in a shorter period of time. Depending on the level of trust, we can move some suppliers through the process more quickly. For example, if a supplier has a history of few rejects, then it may be possible to jump ahead and do five skip lots in order to reach certification. Again, this is something that only you can determine.

PHASE FOUR: Certification

This phase is the easiest to achieve. The first three phases dealt with the efforts required to clarify specifications and establish the testing procedures to receive parts that conform to established requirements. Once this has been performed successfully, we are now ready to certify the supplier for each *specific part number*.

Before the actual presentation of a certification award, we need to review the following for the last time:

• RESULTS OF INSPECTION

• RESULTS OF IN-PLANT MANUFACTURING

• Material Review Board activity

- **Part application audit within the plant**

- **Field return activity**

- **Repairs conducted**

• **CORRECTIVE ACTION**

- **Follow up results of fallout**

- **Documentation follow-up**

- **Bills of material, blueprints, specifications**

• **RESULTS OF PHASE 1, 2, 3**

• **AGREEMENT OF TEAM MEMBERS**

Now that our review has been completed and the entire team is satisfied that all areas have been met, we are ready to certify the supplier for that specific part number which has achieved excellence. Once the supplier is certified, we should acknowledge the achievement with a certificate or some type of ceremony. This can be a letter or plaque. If it is a plaque, we suggest that it be hung on the walls of your lobby, not the supplier's. First, this will be the place where the supplier's competition will view the plaque and hopefully initiate a request to become certified themselves. Second, we want to avoid plaques in a supplier's lobby that announce they were certified ten years ago. Certification is not earned and then forgotten. A supplier must continuously improve to maintain that certification.

Companies have different ideas about certification. Some of them are shortcuts which will not provide us with a long-term position to be competitive. The results we demand are a quality product at the lowest total cost delivered on time. The methods used in the past for building supplier relationships have not been effective. If you are not ready for change, don't try to tackle this issue.

PHASE FIVE: On-going Audit and Maintenance

In Phase 5, we audit and maintain the Supplier Certification program by doing random audits of material and the supplier's process. It helps greatly to designate one person to be responsible for documentation and monitoring the certification process for each supplier. While auditing, this person should take samples from lots and inspect 1) to see that the product meets the print, 2) to see if capability ratios have changed or not, and 3) to see that the supplier's process is under control. You may want to set up a specific frequency for audits.

Disqualification

A supplier loses its certified status if it ships a lot with any discrepancies. In this eventuality, you must alert the supplier with a Memo of Disqualification which outlines the problem and gives suggestions for how it can be solved. Problems will, of course, occur from time to time, but how the supplier handles them makes all the difference. For instance, let's say that a certified supplier informs us that a tool slipped on one of the machines while making parts. He has culled the rejects, fixed the tool and documented precisely what happened. Now, let's say another certified supplier has had a similar problem, but he ships the lot without telling you what happened. Which supplier do you disqualify? The second supplier should be disqualified. He has not demonstrated that his process is under control or that he is interested in being a partner who shares information.

Requalification

After spending many months to achieve a certified status, we believe a supplier deserves some consideration in this area. Our belief is that, once disqualified, a supplier should be given *one* more opportunity to succeed. If disqualified again, then we should start to look for a new source. A certification program must have some teeth in it. Previous supplier programs *did not* show suppliers that we meant business. We sorted, repaired, borrowed and used "as is." Certification means quality from the top of a company to the bottom. Quality is important. Shipping products which do not conform is anathema.

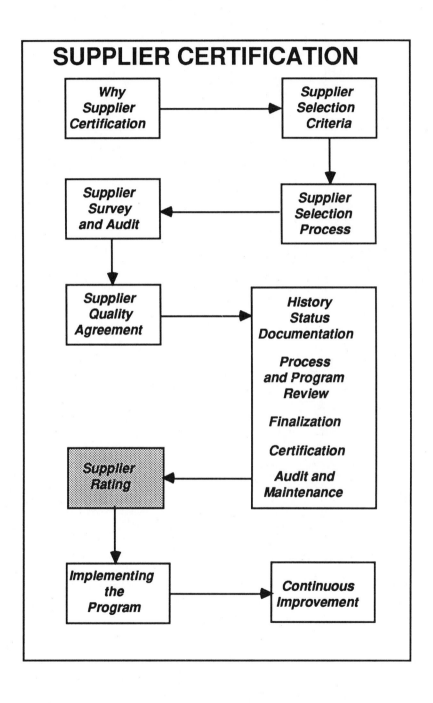

SUPPLIER CERTIFICATION

Why Supplier Certification →	**Supplier Selection Criteria**
Supplier Survey and Audit ←	**Supplier Selection Process**
Supplier Quality Agreement →	**History Status Documentation** **Process and Program Review** **Finalization** **Certification** **Audit and Maintenance**
Supplier Rating ←	
Implementing the Program →	**Continuous Improvement**

SUPPLIER RATINGS

$$=== 7$$

Although many companies rate suppliers before initiating a Supplier Certification program, we view this process as a tool to be used in helping suppliers improve their performance. One of the principal goals of Supplier Certification is to reduce the supplier base, to eliminate those suppliers who are incapable of conforming to our specifications. We must provide all our suppliers the opportunity to become certified. This is a prudent strategy because many suppliers who are presently not performing above the minimum level become significantly better in this program. The incentive to gain a larger share of business and more profit motivates suppliers to improve. Supplier rating is a way for us to determine which suppliers are committed and capable.

Ratings should be performed monthly or at regularly scheduled times. They are designed to help both the customer and the supplier to anticipate and prevent problems with quality, delivery and process control. In this sense, they are very similar to audits which, by definition, are performed after a product is built or a process is completed. As with the criteria described in our supplier survey, rating criteria must also *only* be measurements which can be quantified. We want to avoid situations where suppliers are ranked by "warm and fuzzy" criteria.

For example, cooperation is a desirable result of a Supplier Certification program. How do we quantify this criteria? Do we simply award points because a supplier returns telephone calls? There are more quantitative questions to ask. For instance:

---

1. How many new products have we developed with the supplier?

2. Are corrective actions implemented and documented within 48 hours?

3. How long does it take the supplier to phase in an engineering change?

ELEMENTS REQUIRED FOR A SUPPLIER RATING SYSTEM

Our experience has led us to develop a supplier rating system based on seven elements and two modifiers. As shown here, the

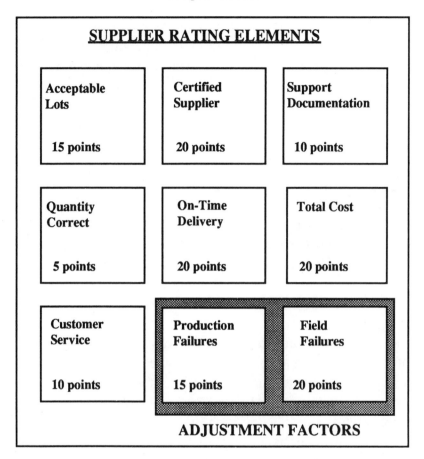

SUPPLIER RATING ELEMENTS

Acceptable Lots	Certified Supplier	Support Documentation
15 points	20 points	10 points
Quantity Correct	On-Time Delivery	Total Cost
5 points	20 points	20 points
Customer Service	Production Failures	Field Failures
10 points	15 points	20 points

ADJUSTMENT FACTORS

emphasis is on quality since Supplier Certification is a quality-oriented program. We recommend that each company assign values according to their importance to the company. For example, if on time delivery is the biggest problem at your plant and quality issues have been eliminated, then we should raise the point value for on time delivery from 20 points to 30. Similarly, if quantities are a problem, we should raise quantity discrepancy from 5 points to 10 or 15. Neither do we need to use the same point values or criteria for all commodities or suppliers. We can devise rating systems by commodity or class of suppliers and we can phase in criteria which may be critical to one supplier and not another. The point is to develop a rating system which we can use as a tool to make the supplier better. Whatever measurements we use, however, should be aimed at improvement, not at maintaining the status quo.

DEFINITIONS OF THE ELEMENTS

Before we explain how to use the rating system and its results, let's first look at the elements in more detail and how to assign points for different supplier actions.

ACCEPTABLE LOTS — Maximum Points = 15

This element measures the percentage of acceptable lots to total lots submitted by a supplier. As we said earlier, a supplier who notifies us of a discrepancy, documents the error and initiates corrective action may not be penalized. The same holds true for a supplier who requests a deviation ahead of shipment. However, a supplier who requests a deviation after production has begun should receive far less points than the supplier in the first example. Our aim is to encourage communication between suppliers and customers before action is taken. If we return the product, the supplier receives no points.

CERTIFIED SUPPLIER — Maximum Points = 20

A rating of 20 points signifies that the supplier is certified for that component or process. If a supplier is in Phase 1 of the program, it would receive 5 points and so on as the chart below suggests:

PHASE	RATING
Not in program	0
Phase 1	5
Phase 2	10
Phase 3	15
Phase 4	20

SUPPORT DOCUMENTATION — Maximum Points = 10

This rating element measures the presence and quality of documentation, certification data, inspection/test results and instruction manuals for operations and maintenance. The more complete this material is, the greater the number of points the supplier receives. Lack of proper documentation received on time should result in zero points. Examples of support documentation are a control chart or metallurgical, chemical and various other data. This support documentation should never replace TQC, however.

QUANTITY CORRECT — Maximum Points = 5

Quite simply, this element measures how close the quantity

shipped is to what was requested. We need to establish a scale which indicates the level of tolerance. Plus or minus 10% is no longer tolerable in a JIT/TQC factory. Suppliers who ship orders with this margin of error should receive zero points. Suppliers who ship with 100% accuracy receive 5 points.

ON TIME DELIVERY — Maximum Points = 20

This element measures on time delivery and the tolerance level within which a supplier must ship product to the plant. The closer a supplier is to delivering products within a specified window, the more points are given. Those suppliers who can deliver on time, 100% of the time, will be given 20 points.

TOTAL COST — Maximum Points = 20

This element should be measured by determining all the costs associated with a supplier's product, not price alone. Then, using the profit equation, we determine what level those costs should be in order to earn a fair profit. How close a supplier comes to paring down costs to the level we set determines the number of points received. Suppliers with costs that exceed this level will have the most points taken away from the total allowed.

CUSTOMER SERVICE — Maximum Points = 10

Here we are looking for suppliers who cooperate and communicate and who meet certain interface requirements. The less cooperative in the following areas, the fewer points are awarded:

- **Lack of Research and Development**
- **Lack of design support**
- **Non-sharing of testing methods**

- **Infrequent and incomplete progress reports**
- **Withholding of technical information**
- **Insufficient assistance in problem-solving**
- **Poor timing — assistance too late**
- **Applicability — assistance not pertinent to subject**

As a customer, you must determine which of the above areas affects you the most. If you are in a growing or a high-tech industry, you may assign more value to Research and Development.

ADJUSTMENT FACTORS

The following two adjustment factors provide a means to take away points for both process and field failures. If you elect to use a demerit program, you would add points to the supplier's total. For a merit program, you would take away point value.

PRODUCTION FAILURES — Maximum Points = 15

This adjustment measures the inherent reliability of a supplier's production. It is a moving average calculation of manufacturing failures. In order to support shipments being delivered to Work-In-Process, a system of production failure feedback must be in place. The production area must report defects which should carry a severe penalty.

FIELD FAILURES — Maximum Points = 20

This adjustment measures the operating reliability of a supplier's product in the field. It isolates and detects field failures and their related costs directly to the supplier. As with production failures, ratings for field failures should be severe and may be reason for a supplier to lose its certified status. Every effort must be made to eliminate field failures.

HOW TO USE THE SUPPLIER RATING CHART

If we use the preceding elements to rate a number of companies, we now have a way to objectively compare the performance of one supplier against another. We now have the basis for a report card which can be sent out to our suppliers. Such a report card for a particular product would look like the chart below:

ELEMENT	MAX. PTS.	RATINGS		
		A	B	C
Acceptable lots	15	12	6	5
Certified supplier	20	15	9	2
Support documentation	10	8	6	6
Quantity correct	5	4	2	1
On-time delivery	20	14	12	9
Total cost	20	13	8	7
Customer Service	10	8	5	4
Totals	100	74	48	34
% of business		60%	20%	20%

We would send this report card to each of the suppliers. Supplier A's report would get the ratings of B and C, its competition, but the suppliers would not be identified by name. This chart makes it clear to each company where they stand in relation to other suppliers and where they stand in each category. We then make it clear to everybody that if they want a larger percentage of business, they must improve their supplier ratings with respect to their competition. In other words, supplier B and C must be better than A to get more business. For supplier A to keep this percentage, however, he cannot stand still. He, too, must improve.

As the report card reads now, supplier C is in danger of losing business or being removed from the supplier base. But, if six months from now the results read as A=74, B=48 and C=74, then supplier A is in danger of losing his share of business. He still has a high total, but it has not changed in six months. In such a case, we must begin to doubt his ability to improve on a continuous basis which is the foundation of a Supplier Certification program. This measurement of supplier performance must press for continuous improvement.

A similar chart can be used to compare a supplier's performance from month to month:

ELEMENT	MAX. PTS.	MONTHS											
Supplier: _____		1	2	3	4	5	6	7	8	9	10	11	12
Acceptable lots	15												
Certified supplier	20												
Support documentation	10												
Quantity correct	5												
On-time delivery	20												
Total cost	20												
Customer Service	10												
Totals	100												
% of business													

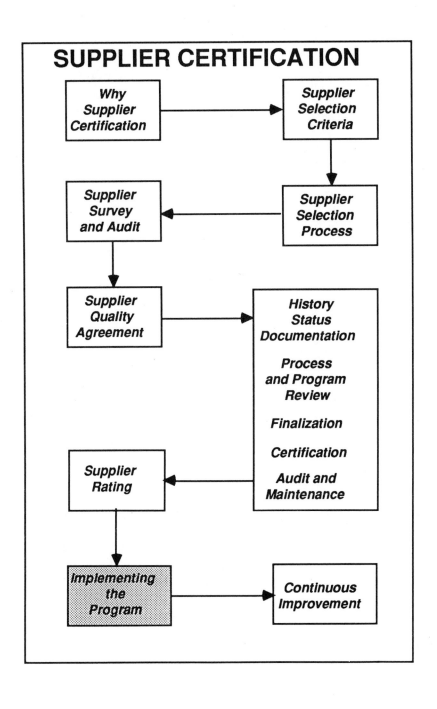

SUPPLIER CERTIFICATION

Why Supplier Certification → **Supplier Selection Criteria**

Supplier Survey and Audit ← **Supplier Selection Process**

Supplier Quality Agreement → **History Status Documentation**

Process and Program Review

Finalization

Certification

Audit and Maintenance

Supplier Rating

Implementing the Program → **Continuous Improvement**

IMPLEMENTING THE PROGRAM

8

The most successful way to implement a Supplier Certification program is to gain top management commitment. Total cost, not standard cost or purchase price, is the important criterion. There are three ways in which we can make management listen. One way is to forward articles, books, reports and pieces of information about the tangible benefits of JIT to the top levels of our companies. A second way is to arrange for on-site visits to plants which have embraced JIT so management can see a Total Business Concept in action. Jerry Claunch and Peter Grieco remember that there were so many requests for visits to the Kawasaki and Apple Macintosh plants when they worked there that a limit had to be imposed. Michael Gozzo was also witness to the commitment companies are giving to Supplier Certification programs when he was involved with Sterling Engineered Products. Sterling was a certified supplier in the Ford Motor Company's "Quality is Number One" program. The third way is to select a small part of the company and implement a pilot project before tackling the whole company.

In the case of the last suggestion, we recommend choosing an area with the most visible paybacks. It could be an area which is most in need of improvement and/or it could be one in which you are assured of success. One way to locate such an area is to use a Pareto approach. By listing all the parts used in manufacturing a product, we will generally find that a relatively small number of items and suppliers account for a large percentage of the product cost. At one client, we were able to free up 35% of the total warehouse space simply by certifying the "A" parts first and getting the suppliers to deliver them as the client needed them. Almost immediately, the champions of the certification program could point to some impressive results.

There is a fourth way to get management commitment. When our Professionals for Technology Associates Director, Phil Stang, C.P.I.M., addresses this last method with clients or at seminars, he uses the following story to make his point:

> Two business people, one Japanese and one American, are at an international manufacturing conference held in Africa. One afternoon, they decide to explore a nearby national game park. They drive up to the entrance where there are signs everywhere: DON'T FEED THE ANIMALS, DON'T LEAVE YOUR VEHICLE,

DANGEROUS WILDLIFE, DON'T DRIVE
OFF THE ROAD.

They drive into the park and they see a herd of
elephants bathing in a pool of water. They both
agree that they must take a photograph of this
sight so they drive the car closer to get a better
picture.

Both of them snap away happily, but when they
return to the car they see that it is stuck in the
mud. After several attempts, they realize that

they won't ever get the car unstuck, so they
decide to walk back to the entrance.

They take their cameras and their suitcases and
start trudging back. As they make the final turn
in the road, they see a pride of lions lying on the
road just ahead of them. The American starts
shaking in his boots, but the Japanese sits down
and starts putting on a pair of sneakers.

The American looks at him as though he's crazy
and says, "You can't outrun those lions!"

"I don't have to," replies the Japanese. "I just
have to stay one step ahead of you, the competition."

Competition is certainly an excellent impetus to get top management commitment for a Supplier Certification program. It is an
undeniable fact that a company looks to its leaders for direction.
Middle management is always ready to embrace a program if
upper management is committed. People at lower levels in the
company are ready to accept change, provided that they are given
the responsibility and authority to act and that there is direction
from above. But, we need to overcome accepted practices which
have conditioned top management to make all the decisions. A
certification program requires suppliers and, in some cases, the
supplier's suppliers to work as a *TEAM*.

A SUPPLIER PARTNERSHIP

We have discovered in our work with clients (in industries such as
food processing, cosmetics, pharmaceuticals, etc.) from around

the world that there are seven objectives in the process of creating a partnership with suppliers:

- Reduce set-up times.
- Increase frequency of deliveries.
- Eliminate waste in supplier's plant.
- Develop inventory turn objectives.
- Seek simplicity in solutions.
- Work for continuous improvement.
- Communicate results and make them visible.

This is the foundation upon which you will create a sense of teamwork. At a recent seminar, we came across a perfect example of a company trying to become certified in a Supplier Certification program. We were pleasantly surprised to see the vice president of this company at our seminar on Supplier Certification. Most of the other participants were representatives of companies that wanted to implement a certification program. This vice president, however, represented a supplier that wanted to know what Supplier Certification was and, most importantly, how to work with a company requesting its suppliers to become certified.

The vice president agreed with the above objectives. He saw the value of working as a team with the company he was supplying. We cite this example because many companies believe that suppliers will automatically balk when asked to meet the above objectives. They won't as long as both the supplier and the manufacturer work together.

At the same time these objectives are being assimilated and becoming second nature through education and open discussion at the supplier's, we should be setting objectives like the ones below at our own company and at our supplier's company:

THE TEN-STEP PLAN

1. Avoid studying or planning a project to death.

2. Don't be satisfied with early successes.

3. Don't get tangled up in techniques.

4. Always strive for continuous improvements.

5. Make problems, goals and accomplishments visible to all.

6. Document all steps of your process.

7. Believe in "small is beautiful" and frequent deliveries.

8. Eliminate waste in your plant and supplier's plant.

9. Seek simplicity in solutions.

10. Develop inventory turn objectives, not stocking programs.

Once these common objectives are established, both internally and externally, we are ready to begin the implementation process of a Supplier Certification program.

THE TOTAL BUSINESS CONCEPT (TBC) APPROACH TO IMPLEMENTATION

In a certification program, it doesn't matter so much which suppliers start the process of implementation, only that we start. The key to the creation of a framework of continuous improvement is teamwork. The implementation and achievement of Supplier Certification consists of four activities:

1. Top Management Commitment

2. Team Administration

3. Training and Education

4. Interdepartmental Cooperation

Only minimal expenditures are needed to improve communication, to involve the workforce in problem-solving and decision-making, or to develop interdepartmental cooperation. And since direct labor will work with management on teams, there is an opportunity for both to learn how to work together. With this level of cooperation, learning curves are quickly diminished, thus lowering total cost.

In effect, the creation of a company culture fosters vision, responsibility, authority and accountability. We can think of the above activities as four pillars which support a roof. Take away one pillar and the structure crashes to the ground.

Thus, a certification program is really no more than a commitment to continuous improvement. To get there means taking what we call the Total Business Concept approach, a journey from exposure through orientation and education to program review and ongoing support. The chart on the opposite page shows this approach.

The left side of the chart shows the preparation phase. It consists of three steps:

> **Orientation and Education** — communicate a consistent message about the program throughout the company.

> **Opportunities** — identify where opportunities exist and what benefits will ensue.

> **Action Plan** — develop a one-year plan (not a five-year plan which will be reviewed every six months) which shows the directions, objectives and goals for success.

Management's involvement in this phase is to provide guidance, vision and direction to the implementation teams.

The right side of the chart is the Implementation Process phase which consists of six steps. In step one, we form teams that are required to address issues in the process. The next step is to

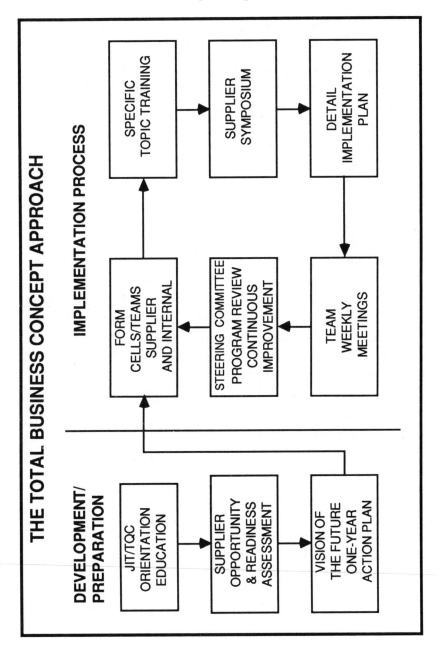

THE TOTAL BUSINESS CONCEPT APPROACH

IMPLEMENTATION PROCESS

SPECIFIC TOPIC TRAINING

SUPPLIER SYMPOSIUM

DETAIL IMPLEMENTATION PLAN

FORM CELLS/TEAMS SUPPLIER AND INTERNAL

STEERING COMMITTEE PROGRAM REVIEW CONTINUOUS IMPROVEMENT

TEAM WEEKLY MEETINGS

DEVELOPMENT/ PREPARATION

JIT/TQC ORIENTATION EDUCATION

SUPPLIER OPPORTUNITY & READINESS ASSESSMENT

VISION OF THE FUTURE ONE-YEAR ACTION PLAN

provide each team specific training in group dynamics and problem-solving. In the third step, the individual teams decide on a course of action that is required to meet the parameters set by a steering committee. Next, we hold a supplier symposium to determine which suppliers are capable of and willing to undergo the certification process which we then detail in the next step. The fifth step is to schedule weekly team meetings where problems are discussed and potential solutions are weighed. The results and activities of these meetings are then passed on to the steering committee which will direct the review activities.

The point of these six steps is to keep the process on-going, so that there is continuous improvement. This is the responsibility of the steering committee which should be comprised of the chairpeople of managerial staff. The steering committee should meet at least once a month. Its purpose is only to report on progress and to check that team efforts are on track. It does not meet to grant permission to teams so that they can start solving problems. The purpose of the Total Business Concept approach to implementation is to focus the whole program at the operator level. We must remind ourselves that these are the people who know best how to identify and solve production problems.

EDUCATION AND TRAINING

Education, of course, is critical to the attainment of Supplier Certification. Our approach to education differs from the norm. We propose that top management spend more time in the education process than the rest of the plant as we have depicted in the educational pyramid shown on the opposite page.

The inverted pyramid emphasizes that top management must be committed to education — learning the theory behind what you

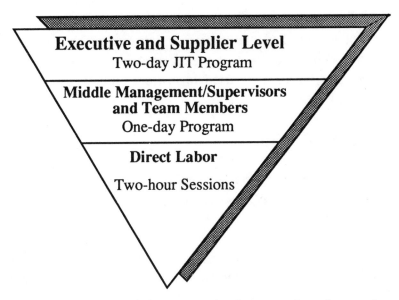

Executive and Supplier Level
Two-day JIT Program

Middle Management/Supervisors and Team Members
One-day Program

Direct Labor
Two-hour Sessions

are doing — and to training, or putting into practice what you have learned.

Although education must occur at all levels of a company as well as in the supplier's plant, top management should receive more extensive education because without their understanding and commitment, the program will encounter difficulties. It is an undeniable fact that workers look to their leaders for direction. A middle manager is far more apt to embrace JIT/TQC if she sees a vice president genuinely committed to it.

Training is a tool to help business meet its objectives today and in the future. Our goal is to provide a positive atmosphere which will stimulate employees to discuss theory, practices and alternatives. We should base training on a competency model identifying each person or function needed as we explained in our book, *JUST-IN-TIME PURCHASING: In Pursuit of Excellence.* Training and education must become a way of life. Some companies, for example, always have structured activities for their workers whenever a line shuts down. We recommend that when a machine is down that the time be used to instruct employees in more problem-solving techniques.

WHAT IS A TEAM?

>*A team is a group dedicated to a common goal.*
>*Its members rely on each other's strengths and*
>*fill in for each other's weaknesses.*

The results of a team will be greater than the sum of efforts made by individuals. As we pointed out in our book, *MADE IN AMERICA: The Total Business Concept*, much of JIT has a gestalt, or holistic, effect. Even though a company is made up of autonomous parts, they add up to a whole. Teams are similar in that they are made up of individuals from a number of disciplines within a company and from its suppliers. Thus, when a team sets out to solve a problem, there are inputs from a number of areas, each of which states how possible solutions will affect them. Hypotheses and plans of action are made by a group process.

TEAM STRUCTURE
AND MEMBER SELECTION

The first step in team-building is to form a steering committee. The steering committee should be an interdepartmental team consisting of six to eight people from the areas of Engineering, Design, Sales, Marketing, Production, Purchasing and Finance. It would also be wise to include a union person to impress upon members the importance and necessity of flexibility in a union environment. For non-union plants, include a direct labor person.

The steering committee involves itself in the preparatory phase of the JIT journey:

1. Exposure to JIT through orientation and education.

2. Preparation of an opportunity and readiness assessment in terms of talent internal and external to your company.

3. Development of a future company vision and first year action plan through planning sessions.

The steering committee then discusses what teams should be formed in this implementation phase of the Total Business Concept approach. Project teams, as the name implies, coalesce around certain projects brought to their attention by the steering committee. When starting a typical implementation project, we recommend four to five teams of 6-10 people to be established as a pilot.

The actual rules or plans of action are the job of a team working within the guidelines established by the steering committee. The steering committee is the catalyst. It defines what JIT means to the company, reviews projects, provides resources and guides the overall effort toward continuous improvement. Another way to put this is to say that the steering committee creates the culture for change and maintains that environment.

If the steering committee is the strategy maker, then the team finds ways to implement that strategy. Any team, then, really has only one overall mandate — investigate symptoms, identify the causes (problems), identify the means to solve the problem and implement the lowest cost solution which eliminates the problem.

The composition of a JIT team should be 50% direct labor and 50% management from both the supplier and your company. Certainly, we need people on the team with expertise. We also need some people with little knowledge but with the ability to never be satisfied. There is something to be said for "naive" members, the ones who ask all the "dumb" questions. For example: "Why do you do it this way?" We call this team process, DSE, or Different Set of Eyes. Such a person has the ability to maintain an insight which is consistently fresh. That's the type of person we want on a team.

Selecting team members with fresh insight is one way to break down existing barriers in a company. Another way is to expose JIT teams to the full range of problems. The idea behind teamwork is to expand the base of experience, so that no one team, for example, becomes known as the team responsible for set-up reduction. Thus, we should make sure that set-up problems are identified on each team. The same holds true for other problems such as communication, morale, safety, preventive maintenance, quality, etc.

Besides the ability to question, team members must be given the proper decision-making authority and responsibility to make change happen. Since teams will ideally have both direct labor and

management, we will have to demonstrate that we are working as a team. Giving direct labor equal representation is effective in encouraging participation, overcoming workers' fears and fostering trust in management. In short, the same non-adversarial quality which determines supplier relationships should also determine the relationship between management and direct labor.

TEAM RULES AND OBJECTIVES

There are inherent problems with teams. Whenever a lot of cooks are stirring the broth, there will be arguments over what ingredients are best. How do you form and manage a team in which you reap the benefits of a diverse group while not stifling individual creativity? How can Purchasing sit down with Marketing, Engineering, Production and Quality and come up with integrated solutions? How do you create a team?

The answer comes in four parts. One, we need to establish ground rules, goals, objectives and a sense of direction. Two, we need to educate and train all levels of your company and your supplier's in JIT. Three, we must teach teams how to administer the formation and implementation of the action plans. Four, we must initiate program reviews and provide on-going support. All of these four parts are done both internally and externally through the creation of a partnership with your suppliers and people.

PERFORMANCE MEASUREMENTS

How do we know if we are succeeding? That is the question that must be addressed. We measure performance in order to be predictable, so that we know where we have been, where we are and where we are going. It is possible to measure the wrong areas as is pointed out by the authors, H. Thomas Johnson and Robert S. Kaplan, in *RELEVANCE LOST*. Director Mel Pilachowski of Professionals for Technology Associates says that the problem with the old yardsticks of performance is that they are not looking at total cost solutions. They look only at productivity levels and use a reactive, rather than a proactive approach.

Today, we must use new yardsticks which provide information to make decisions. Then, we will be able to compare actual data against predicted performance. This gives us the opportunity to take corrective action. This is the definition of proactive: to measure the predictability of the outcomes of decision-making in real time.

This is best accomplished through a system of measurement that reflects a Total Business Concept. In general, the use of TBC measurements will show:

1. How close we are to having on-line, real-time information about both internal and external manufacturing operations as well as purchasing activities. Current information coupled with supplier involvement will provide a new approach.

2. How accurate our information is. We all know that a small mistake compounds over time. Unlike interest on your personal investments, this is not favorable. The surveyor who makes a mistake of one degree can cost you many valuable acres of land.

3. How much waste is present in manufacturing and supplier operations and purchasing activities. Waste, today, is too often accepted as a given and absorbed into overhead costs. This is truly a reactive way of thinking and must change as we compete in a world market.

4. How actual performance compares to the stated plan. Observing this variance is instrumental in making new plans which take corrective action. Those who don't learn from the mistakes of the past are doomed to repeat them.

These new yardsticks are based on total cost. In essence, Pilachowski points out, this is the same as measuring the performance of the whole company. Our principal thrust should be to emphasize a total cost-oriented, rather than a price-oriented, approach in financial measurements, an approach which attempts to gain financial control through cost improvement.

There are two principles behind cost improvement. One, we should not look at price alone in seeking to maximize profits, but also look at quality, quantity and delivery. Two, we should measure variances against cost, not price, when evaluating our profitability. These two principles work in tandem with the basic principles of JIT/TQC; that is, build to demand and eliminate excess inventory and wasteful operations. This concept is a change from one of the present measurements of today, Purchase Price Variance, which is employed by many organizations.

As we streamline our plant through the reduction of costs, we find that Finance's job actually becomes easier as accountability is built into the process of manufacturing. For example, Finance's accounting of inventory becomes easier when we eliminate buffers, safety stocks, queues and lead times. In the JIT/TQC environment, inventory can be accounted for merely by looking at prescribed levels of Work-In-Process. By giving up traditional manufacturing and accounting practices, we will have more control than before.

An overall measurement of the success of our certification program is the number of suppliers who are participating. The number of participants alone is not as important as how many part numbers are included. We should have a high percentage for those

25% of our suppliers which account for 90-95% of the process or part number. The goal is to have 100% of your suppliers shipping 100% quality components with 100% on-time delivery in accurate quantities 100% of the time.

THE SUPPLIER CERTIFICATION AUDIT

To help in the area of performance measurements, we have developed an audit procedure to assess the implementation of Supplier Certification. This audit is discussed at length in *JUST-IN-TIME PURCHASING: In Pursuit of Excellence*, but we list some here to give you an idea of what a TBC measurement is. There are, of course, no right or wrong answers to this audit. The point is to show that there is always room for improvement.

Throughput

**What percentage of your total inventory
has been sold? _____%**

Throughput measures the total amount of production which has been sold. If you bought enough material and components to build 100 products, built 80, have enough material to build 20 more in queue, and stored 10 units in finished goods inventory, your throughput percentage is 70%. Traditional methods would not detect the 30 units either in production or waiting to be sold. They may indicate that the throughput level is at 80, 90 or even 100%, since there is no material left in the storeroom. But, a TBC measurement makes no distinctions (as far as the bottom line goes) between material in a queue or in finished goods. The criterion here is simply how much you sell. If you are overproducing, this measurement tells you so. It may indicate that you are not building to demand, that your company is still operating in a "push," rather than a "pull," environment.

Reduced Set-Up Times

By what percentage have your suppliers and plant reduced set-up times? ____ %

Set-up time is the amount of time it takes to change over a work center from the production of one item to another item. It is measured from the point where the last good product was produced for item #1 to the first good product of item #2 and should include the time it takes the operator to get the machine to full efficiency. Set-up time is one of the first areas to attack in reducing lead times. It is also a highly visible area which can act as a great motivator to the implementation of further JIT practices. For example, we have a client who was able to reduce one set-up time from 35 minutes to 9 seconds. Recognition of that fact only serves to make people want to reduce the set-up times at their work centers by similar percentages.

It is quite evident that reduced set-up times increase the production rate and subsequently lower inventory levels as well as unlocking capacity which used to be wasted in excess and obsolete inventory. Another equally valid result is the ability now for production lines to be much more flexible and to reduce lot sizes. This, in turn, allows you to come closer and closer to building products based on actual demand without storing excess inventory.

Ship-to-WIP vs. Ship-to-Stock

What percentage of your procured material is shipped directly to Work-In-Process? ____% To stock? ___%

This measurement presupposes that you first have excellent quality and on time delivery to your receiving area. If you do not, refer to the next measurement described. Material delivered to WIP is ready to be consumed; it does not sit in storage or queues adding inventory carrying costs to your bottom line. Supplier Certification will contribute to achievements in this area.

On Time Delivery

What percentage of supplier deliveries are on time? ___%
How is on time delivery measured to the delivery date? +/- __
hours +/- __ one day +/- __ five days __other (explain)

On time delivery compares the actual receipt date to the supplier's committed delivery date based on shop need. This is obviously an important measurement being that JIT manufacturing relies on Just-In-Time delivery from suppliers. Remember, however, that early delivery is just as costly as late delivery. If you're receiving parts two or three days ahead of schedule, inventory will rise. The higher the percentage of suppliers delivering on time and the smaller your delivery window, the closer you come to JIT purchasing. This is a measurement which needs to be calculated for delivery as a whole and for each individual supplier. Improvement is gained as more and more suppliers come over to JIT delivery.

Inventory Turnover Ratio

How many inventory turns do you get a year? ___ #/yr

The inventory turnover ratio is the forecasted cost of goods sold over the next twelve months divided by the inventory investment.

$$ITR = \frac{\text{Forecasted Cost of Goods}}{\text{Inventory Investment}}$$

In our book, *MADE IN AMERICA: The Total Business Concept,* we noted that the measurement of total inventory turns is perhaps the single best method for determining the progress of JIT/TQC implementation. Inventory turnovers are something like the Dow Jones Industrial Average in that both act as an overall indicator of the movements of many variables. In the case of the Dow, these variables are 30 leading industrial companies. In the case of the ITR, these variables are associated with lot sizing, inventory management, line balancing and the Theory of One. We can increase inventory turns by planning for only as much material as a work station needs to make one product and by minimizing queues so that a work station has only enough material to make a product in its cycle time.

Most companies today are struggling to achieve three inventory turns a year. This means they carry four months of inventory. We have worked with companies that have raised the level to 14 turns, 26 turns, 36 turns, even 42 turns a year. Obviously, these companies have been able to coordinate many of the variables mentioned in the paragraph above. Purchasing, once again, can lead the way in the struggle to achieve a higher inventory turnover rate.

A COMPANY-WIDE PERSPECTIVE

If you have noted one dominant theme in our discussion on measurements, it must be the theme of interrelationship. By measuring one area in a JIT environment, you are in effect measuring how well the whole of your company is working. Quality, for example, is also measured by on time delivery. You don't have an on time delivery if there are defective parts in the shipment. As another example, let's consider the time it takes to process engineering change orders. Surely, this indicates how well your company is working as a team, but it also indicates how well your relationship with suppliers is working. Remember that earlier, we emphasized that engineering changes are as vital to your suppliers as they are to your production department. After all, suppliers are shipping the material from which you make your product.

REWARDS

How do we reward suppliers who are performing excellently? We recommend that you ask your suppliers and employees what they want as a realistic reward. Management often finds this topic difficult because it is hard to know what satisfies everybody. All the more reason, then, to involve the team in the process of selecting a reward system. With employees, rewards may come as money, recognition or both. With suppliers, it might be payment terms or cash for on time delivery. Money may be a better reward than any plaque or certificate, but that is not to say that we should not recognize excellence with a more visible reward.

We have a client who placed an advertisement in the local

newspaper of one of its suppliers. The piece praised the company for achieving Supplier Certification and for the high level of its quality and delivery.

The end product of JIT teams is ideas or recommendations with accompanying action plans. And recognition must be more than unlocking a "suggestion box" and awarding one prize for the best idea while throwing the other ideas into the round file. The best run companies in America are willing to follow through on ideas which may end in failure. These companies are not afraid to include the word "failure" in their vocabulary. Peter Grieco has said, "A person needs the opportunity to fail in order to succeed."

Thus, your company needs to create an environment where it is safe to make suggestions. No suggestion, no question, is unimportant. Toyota Motor Corporation, for example, has developed a suggestion system in which its non-management 55,000-strong work force contributed over 2.649 million improvement proposals in 1986. The Mazda Company in 1987 received 350,000 suggestions from its 800 employees. Obviously, it is safe to suggest changes in these companies. Besides having an open-minded attitude, these companies also act quickly on the given suggestions. Every idea is distributed to the appropriate team or department for action. In addition, we recommend taking "bad" suggestions (which may be suggestions which are not clearly described) and using them in training sessions where you teach company employees how to make more effective suggestions.

CONCLUSION

Progress toward the goal of a successful implementation begins with this assessment:

What are we doing and why are we doing it?

Only when this question is constantly asked will a company be on its way to improvement. Top management commitment means building an environment where creative problem-solving is the norm. Furthermore, it means squarely confronting the most difficult task of management—listening to people. This can be accomplished if management first establishes goals and objectives and exercises patience and persistence in working with people. It will require the development of trust with your people, suppliers and customers and the delegation of responsibility and authority to the lowest levels of the organization. You will know you are there when you can demonstrate the following actions:

- Establish an on going training and education program.

- Adopt a no-waste attitude.

- Allocate/authorize financial support and measurements.

- Devote resources to project teams.

- Risk short-term operational results for long-term improvements.

- Foster interdepartmental communication and cooperation.

- Follow up, monitor, document and measure.

- Improve communications with suppliers and customers.

- Listen to the experts—your people.

- Correct processes, rather than rework parts.

- Foster a "no-waiver" environment in processes and specifications.

There is no question in our minds that Supplier Certification will work when this mind-set is employed. The next challenge will be to make all this fit into Computer Integrated Manufacturing (CIM). The complex problems which face us in the future cry out for more improvements and higher profits. Supplier Certification is a step toward the goal of internal and external control. Don't get trapped into thinking that this a supplier's problem. Many suppliers' problems are ultimately caused by the customer (you)!

A Supplier Certification program requires commitment and time. Patience is important and so is doing it right the first time.

SUPPLIER CERTIFICATION

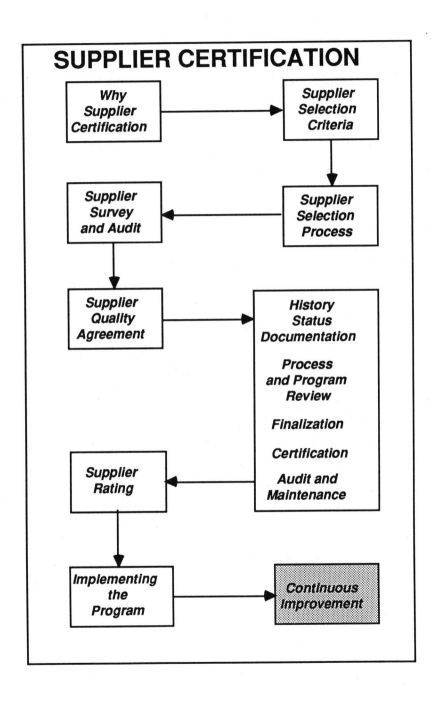

DOING BUSINESS WITH THE GOVERNMENT

9

The procurement problems at the Pentagon are only the tip of the government's problem obtaining quality material at the lowest cost. The entire process of selecting suppliers and ensuring quality is riddled with outdated, inefficient and costly procedures. By focusing on products, such as hammers which cost $600, critics of government programs are falling into the same trap as the government. It is not the price and quality of products that the government should be concerned about, but the quality and control of processes at their suppliers' plants. Supplier Certification is the only way the government can begin to address these issues. In fact, the government would be wise to observe those companies which have embraced the new orientation toward certifying the supplier's process, rather than inspecting finished goods.

The first obstacle for the government to overcome is the entrenched bureaucracy present in most of its departments and agencies. Somebody in the executive branch, perhaps the President himself, has to take charge and make a commitment to ridding our government's procurement system of traditional and inefficient procedures. Once that commitment has been made, it is then necessary to educate and train an "overworked" and inadequately trained staff in the philosophy and application of Supplier Certification. This commitment to revamping procurement practices should pertain to all departments and agencies which purchase material for the government. In other words, there shouldn't be one system for the Department of Defense and another for the Food and Drug Administration. Part of the problem has been a sort of Tower of Babel approach to procurement by our government. Everybody speaks a different language. When a supplier to the government needs several "interpreters" to understand the mass of governmental regulations, then it should come as no surprise that costs escalate.

Anybody who has looked at government manuals issued to suppliers is aware of a plethora of paragraphs and sub-paragraphs stating procedures and specifications which must be adhered to. You would think by the sheer mass of information that the government is doing a good job of controlling every detail. By fixing its attention on the details, however, it has seen the trees, but missed the forest. These manuals fail to achieve quality at the supplier's plant because they emphasize picayune procedures over the control of processes. The government has constructed a system which guarantees that suppliers will produce excellent paperwork *and* faulty components.

The government makes two mistakes when it formulates specifications for products. First, it draws up specifications for the inspection of finished products, rather than designing specifications for controlling a process. Second, it overspecifies. Specifications are not determined by customer need. The government wrongly believes that by tightening specifications, it is ensuring quality. Quite the opposite is true. In a Supplier Certification environment, specifications conform to customer requirements. It seems, for example, that a soldier could get by with a $20 hammer off the shelf as well as he could with one costing thirty times more. There are, of course, some products that the government buys which require the most technically feasible specifications possible. Parts for the space shuttle, for example. In other words, conformance to customer requirements varies according to the criticality of the part or material being purchased. Supplier Certification recognizes this need and assures us of the highest quality and safety when this is truly the demand of the customer. The criteria used for buying space shuttle parts, for example, need not be the criteria we use to buy hammers or toilet seats.

These manuals, especially the MIL standards put out by the Department of Defense, are also oriented toward an Acceptable Quality Level (AQL) rather than a Certified Quality Level (CQL). As we have noted before, an AQL approach allows defects. In fact, a 2% AQL says that two parts out of every 100 will be bad. Total Quality Control does not accept anything less than 100% quality and achieves that level by being statistically driven. There must be more emphasis in government documents of Statistical Process Control (SPC), a cornerstone of Supplier Certification. With SPC, the emphasis is on controlling the suppliers' process and making them responsible for producing quality parts. If machines are so well maintained and controlled that they never produce bad parts, then 100% quality becomes a far easier goal to achieve as it eliminates wasteful paperwork and red tape. In fact, the government would find that far more suppliers would be willing to do work for the government if they did not have to jump through so many hoops.

EXAMPLES OF GOVERNMENT REGULATIONS

MIL-STD-45662

In the Department of Defense's MIL-STD-45662 for calibration systems requirements, there is no mention of using statistical methods to control the accuracy of measuring and test equipment. Here is a perfect example of what we just mentioned. Furthermore, the emphasis on merely defining standards instead of process control is vague. It leaves the determination of how to control accuracy up to the individual supplier. Thus, the government must send in inspectors to determine if the job is being done correctly. And, of course, every supplier will be different, which makes the government's role even more difficult. This emphasis on inspection should be replaced by one program which applies to every supplier. That program utilizes statistical control and puts the responsibility for quality at the supplier's door.

It may be nitpicking, but the fact that there is a spelling mistake in this document does set a tone. At the top of the third page, in capital letters, is the word "FORWARD." Obviously, what they meant to put was "FOREWORD." It makes one wonder about the level of quality control in their own department. Remember: what you demand from a supplier, you must also demand of yourself.

MIL-Q-9858A

This document on quality program requirements states in section 3.5 (Corrective Action) that "the quality program shall detect promptly and correct assignable conditions adverse to quality." That sounds reasonable upon first reading, but a closer reading reveals some problems. Again, it merely states the desired result without mentioning how the process of corrective action should be controlled. Later in the section, it does mention the need to analyze trends in processes. Nowhere, however, does it mention that the purpose of corrective action is not to treat a symptom, but to find and cure the problems which cause the symptoms to appear.

Section 6.1 (Materials and Materials Control) states that all "supplier's materials and products shall be subjected to inspection …" This is unnecessary in a Supplier Certification environment. At the end of the paragraph, it states that "evidence of suppliers' satisfactory control of quality may be used to adjust the amount and kind of receiving inspection." Here is evidence, we think, of the government's reliance on an AQL approach to quality. The answer is not to use less final inspection as a reward, but to eliminate final inspection by controlling the process.

In section 6.6 (Statistical Quality Control and Analysis), the document states that statistical methods "may be utilized when-ever such procedures are suitable to maintain the required control of quality." In our opinion, this is a rather weak endorsement of the engine that drives Supplier Certification and the achievement of 100% quality.

Contractor System Status Review Guide

What can you say about a document over 180 pages long which presents a very complete picture of how to audit a supplier? We have seen documents from our clients that cover the same material in the same depth in less than a fifth of the number of pages the government requires. We also wonder how often this document is actually used and how well trained the people are who conduct the audit. Is this just another instance of overspecification?

Food and Drug Administration (FDA)

In contrast to the above document, there is an 11-page paper issued by the FDA entitled "Good Manufacturing Practices." Here is what it covers:

Organization and Personnel
Buildings
Equipment
Control of Raw Materials
Production and Process Controls
Packaging and Label Control
Holding and Distribution
Product Evaluation
Records

In its 11 pages, this document gets across more about the principles which underlie Supplier Certification than most other government publications. It emphasizes housekeeping and preventive maintenance, education and training, calibration scheduling, SPC and conformance to customer requirements. The FDA, on the basis of this document, seems to be more process oriented than product oriented in its approach to quality. Perhaps this is so because the agency deals with items which are critical to the lives and health of human beings. It goes to show that high levels of quality are achievable if the effort is made.

SUPPLIER CERTIFICATION AS THE SOLUTION

We believe it is clear that the government should adopt a Supplier Certification program as a way of life. Such a program would undoubtedly result in more bang for the taxpayer's buck. Right now, you and I are supporting waste with our hard-earned dollars.

Supplier Certification would also assure us of quality products and do much toward eliminating defense projects which don't work, disasters such as the Challenger and nuclear plants which pollute our environment. It will take hard work and an unrelenting commitment, but it's not impossible.

Recently, for instance, Hughes Aircraft Corporation was authorized by the Department of Defense to deliver tactical display systems without government inspection. Hughes was the first major contractor ever to be given this status. Prior to this certification, Hughes had to submit its final products to the Navy for inspection and approval. Now, having obtained a Certificate of Conformance from the government, the company is able to deliver products based on its own quality certification.

Hughes achieved this level by improving its own quality control and its suppliers'. A Supplier Certification program called Partnership in Excellence (PIE) was started. Top management support was solicited from Hughes' major suppliers and the program was based on detecting defects in the process using statistical methods. Hughes made a commitment to determine the causes of problems, rather than treating symptoms. And, as in the program we have explained in this book, workers were given responsibility and authority for quality. They were also involved in problem-solving.

In the case of Hughes Aircraft, we believe that the government is moving in the right direction. But let's not stop there. Remember that Supplier Certification is also a program of continuous improvement. We want to see that *America* keeps moving ahead.

CASE
STUDIES

$=$ **10**

The following case studies are all derived from actual work done
at clients of Professionals for Technology Associates, Inc. (Pro-
Tech), an international management counseling and education
firm, and from discussions with people knowledgeable in the area
of Supplier Certification. We have attempted to select companies
like yours to which we could pose questions that are uppermost in
the minds of company managers. These are questions about real
situations, questions we think you would want answered.

E.I. DU PONT DE NEMOURS &COMPANY INC.
Imaging Systems Dept.
Towanda, PA

QUESTIONS: 1) How has this Du Pont plant designed its Supplier Certification program? 2) In particular, how has it coordinated internal and external requirements?

ANSWERS: 1) The Towanda plant of Du Pont, according to Phil Taylor of Purchasing, has a vendor certification program in place which subscribes to the first and foremost rule of such programs — recognition of the fact that vendor certification has both an internal and external component. The people responsible for this plant's program have set clearly defined goals and have made considerable progress in achieving those goals.

2) The internal component of the program begins with a set of beliefs. Although drawn up for the Towanda plant, keep in mind that these are also principles to which suppliers should adhere:

> 1. World class status provides a competitive advantage for the Towanda plant and the businesses it serves.

> 2. World class status is attained by unleashing the potential for innovative thinking residing in the plant's people.

> 3. Unity of purpose is the result of open, fair and caring treatment of people.

4. A competitive, high-performance organization relies on output-driven, customer-focused, self-managed teams.

5. Safety is a prerequisite for achieving functional excellence.

6. A total quality approach which emphasizes "doing it right the first time" and "fixing problems at their source" is required to achieve functional and competitive excellence.

7. Continual improvement is the path to long-term economic and global viability. This is attained by upgrading and improving people's skills while implementing state-of-the-art technologies in product, equipment and organizational processes.

8. Setting benchmarks will accelerate our advancement toward world class manufacturing.

The Towanda plant has also based its progress toward world class status on the four pillars of Just-In-Time, Total Quality Control, Employee Involvement and Total Reliability. The company has recognized that a certification program works only when its internal organization is equipped to handle the Just-In-Time delivery of zero-defect parts from its suppliers. To further this end, the plant has adopted the following principles for each area:

JUST-IN-TIME

1. We will only pursue "value-added" activity and eliminate "cost-added" activity.

2. We will audit each process step activity and work to cut:

> Work-In-Process.
> Flow times.
> Set-up and change-over times.
> Flow distances and floor space
> requirements.
> Testing.
> Cycle interval time.
> Product scale-up time.

3. We will release only defect-free material to the next work station.

4. We will promote teamwork between manufacturing operations and all business departments and functional groups.

5. We will promote JIT through education and communication.

6. We will be guided by world class manufacturing concepts in how we plan, design, implement, automate and operate facilities.

TOTAL QUALITY CONTROL

1. We will develop quality performance expectations and goals to measure our ability to meet customer needs.

2. We will treat the problem, not the symptom.

3. We will only ship conforming product.

4. We will provide feedback and assistance to our suppliers regarding quality.

5. We will consistently provide product within specification to the next operation in the process chain.

EMPLOYEE INVOLVEMENT

1. Each employee will accept responsibility and accountability for responding to internal and external requests.

2. Each employee will seek to continually improve his ability to identify and solve problems.

TOTAL RELIABILITY

1. We will understand the cause of failure (statistics or preventive measurement) and take action to prevent problems.

2. We will provide frequent and regular scheduling for preventive maintenance.

As for the suppliers, the Towanda plant expects them to meet or exceed DuPont specification requirements. These expectations are no more than what DuPont demands of itself. For example, suppliers are asked to continually improve product quality and reliability through total and statistical quality control techniques. They are asked to be responsive to corrective action requests and to provide advance notice of any major process and product changes. This is precisely the partnership we have discussed earlier in this book. The actual phases of the certification program also follow the basic five steps we demonstrated earlier as well. The Towanda plant has successfully brought the internal and external components of Supplier Certification together into a synergistic whole.

UNIVERSITY SEMINAR CENTER
Boston, MA

DATA: University Seminar Center presents seminars across the country on topics of interest to business professionals.

QUESTIONS: 1) How popular are Supplier Certification programs? 2) What are the reasons people attend? 3) Is any one group particularly interested? Or, does participation cut across all departments, management levels, industries and company sizes?

ANSWERS: Director of Program Development, Jean Hey, says that the seminar company for which she works has noticed that:

1) Supplier Certification has consistently been one of our most successful seminars since its inception.

2) People want a "nuts-and-bolts" understanding of how to tackle poor quality at its source, that is, with the vendor.

3) Most of our participants are from middle management and come principally from the purchasing and quality control divisions of their companies.

THE CLOROX COMPANY
Pleasanton, CA

QUESTIONS: 1) What are the goals and objectives of Corporate Quality Assurance? 2) How did your company implement its Supplier Certification? 3) How did the suppliers react? 4) How were project teams implemented? Who served on them? How were meetings conducted? 5) How was the program implemented?

ANSWERS: 1) The primary goal of Corporate Quality Assurance (CQA), says John Crossley, Quality Services—Project Leader II, is to consistently assure top quality consumer products through the concept of Total Quality Management. This is in line with our company goal of providing the consumer with only needed quality products.

The plan is to develop within each of the five divisions of Clorox:

> • The necessary statistical tools to measure the production and/or processes.

> • A documented process of transferring products efficiently from R&D to Manufacturing.

> • An on-going quality program that relies on quality built into the process requiring only an audit of production.

> • Support to the production with Supplier Certification, where applicable, that can move to a JIT iteration if needed.

• Cost effective, long-term relationships with a
limited number of suppliers.

Supplier Certification has been driven by CQA based on a need
identified at the design stage of our new plant in Dyersburg, TN.
It resulted from the obvious conclusion that traditional "toll gate"
quality control testing could not be used to release product at the
contemplated production rates.

From this, CQA developed a policy based on in-house experience
and knowledge of current quality thinking (e.g. Statistical Process
Control or SPC).

2) The policy was applied to the Dyersburg plant as a pilot
program which we saw as having a high potential for success. Raw
material suppliers were approached by our Purchasing Department for their interest in Supplier Certification. Teams were
formed and our policy shared with the supplier.

3) The suppliers reacted very positively. They liked our policy
approach, understanding that it was a dynamic process that could
be adjusted if needed. They also liked the statistical measuring
steps that allowed everyone to follow the success of the project
and the emphasis on working out the actual certification steps at
the plant production level. It was interesting to note that most suppliers were at our level of SPC expertise or below. In some cases
they had committed to SPC, but had not implemented it. One
supplier took our project as its pilot program for SPC implementation and now wants to introduce its suppliers to the concepts
contained in our vendor certification policy.

4) CQA requested, as a minimum, that each supplier provide representatives from Quality, Manufacturing, and Sales to the team. Clorox was to provide a similar group made up of Purchasing (the primary contact for all meeting matters), CQA (for all test methods and SPC), Manufacturing, and Division QC. Representatives from process and product development departments were also included. The concept was to have a fluid team membership that would change as the certification process progressed.

Initial meetings are held at the Technical Center. Subsequent meetings, as needed, are at the supplier's technical and/or production facilities or at the Dyersburg plant. The idea is to create a team that will meet where it is most appropriate. To emphasize the team concept, the host company organizes the meeting and leads the discussions.

5) CQA has been responsible for implementing the first two parts of our policy: Test Method Alignment (which includes the mutual agreement on key variables to be measured) and Feasibility (a preliminary statistical evaluation of vendor historical data).

Division QC and the actual production location will drive the final capability phase with the supplier. CQA remains on the team as a resource.

We have currently introduced ten suppliers to our certification policy. Three of these should be certified by January 1989, and the others by March 1989.

COSMAIR, INC.
Piscataway, NJ

QUESTIONS: 1) How do you rate suppliers? 2) How do you define defect?

ANSWERS: 1) Since Cosmair is a complex entity of focused business units, says Manager of Quality Assurance Tom Papp, it was necessary to create one system of rating suppliers. This system was based on Cosmair's commitment to the establishment of consistent methods of procurement, improvement in quality standards, and the development of a partnership with every supplier. Thus, suppliers were rated to determine how far each was progressing toward the goal of "Best in Class."

All suppliers currently doing business with Cosmair were rated in the following areas:

Quality of goods	**40% of rating**
JIT/Service commitment	**30% of rating**
Cost competitiveness	**20% of rating**
Technical abilities	**10% of rating**

Quality of goods rates each delivery of a component, WIP or finished product from a supplier on a scale from 10 to 0. A "10" means that there are zero defects in the shipment. A "0" means that all shipments were rejected. A score of "1" to "9" is given according to the number of defects present and the acceptable levels. Ratings are then averaged on a monthly basis for each supplier.

JIT/Service commitment consists of three items:

- Commitment to cycle time reduction.
- Respect of lead times and delivery commitments.
- Policy of inventory reduction.

Cost competitiveness requirements are:

- Commitment to reducing all non value-added wastes.
- Value analysis programs to reduce costs.
- Breakdown of cost elements (material, labor, overhead, profit).

Technical abilities of suppliers should demonstrate:

- Company-wide processes and facilities.
- Technical innovation/creativity in design.
- Control of secondary operations.

2) Furthermore, Cosmair came up with a standard definition for each of three classes of defects. They are:

Critical Defects A defect which can:
- Cause harm to the consumer.
- Render the item useless.

Major Defects A defect which can:
- Reduce to a major degree the commercial value.
- Reduce the usable/salable value of the item.
- Hinder normal use on line or by the consumer.
- Be defined by limits as aesthetic.

Minor Defects A defect which:
- Has minimal impact on the commercial value.
- Is not likely to reduce usable value or function.
- Exceeds aesthetic limit standards.

With the standardization of ratings and defect definitions, Cosmair and its suppliers speak a common language. That makes it easier to create a partnership and to maintain it.

PROGRESSIVE TECHNOLOGY, INC.
Rocky Hill, CT

QUESTIONS: How does a small company initiate a Supplier Certification program and how do you participate in certification programs of large customers?

ANSWERS: Progressive Technology answered both these questions with one approach. They took the tack that it was necessary to put their own house in order, says Vice President of Engineering John Russo, before they could initiate or participate in a certification program. This meant answering a checklist similar to the one developed by Philip D. Stang of Pro-Tech. The following checklist provides a starting point for an internal review to be conducted by companies, large or small, embarking on a certification program:

1. Does your company "vision" include a commitment to the principles and philosophies of Just-In-Time and Total Quality Control? Does this include involvement from the CEO through the operator levels?

2. Are you committed in both word and action to a Continuous Improvement Program?

3. Is Statistical Process Control utilized in your company as a vehicle for continuous improvement?

4. Do you believe that "zero-defects" can become a reality?

5. Are you ready to **trust** your suppliers, dispensing with "ironclad," penalty-clause contracts in order to achieve true long-term partnerships?

6. Is your company prepared to share information openly with its suppliers? For example, production schedules, financials, design information, etc.

7. Is there a total commitment to the added-value approach to doing business, eliminating waste in all areas?

8. Have you embraced up-to-date accounting and performance measurements which emphasize total cost?

9. Do you understand and practice quality at the source?

10. Do you understand and measure the cost of "un-quality"?

11. Are your specifications in line with your real quality requirements? Do you ever waive non-conforming product as "good enough this time"?

12. Do you have active set-up reduction and preventive maintenance programs in place?

This checklist helps a company reflect on its attitudes toward and readiness for a Supplier Certification program. Progressive Technology soon realized that nothing less than a total commitment was required. Over the months, this small tool and die manufacturer has made significant improvements in quality, delivery time, set-up reduction and inventory control. They have been rewarded by their larger customers with continued purchase orders and have seen a significant rise in orders from new customers who have learned of their reliability and quality. New customers have also been impressed by Progressive Technology's ability to manage its supplier base to ensure the same high levels of reliability and quality.

RICOH CORPORATION
San Jose , CA

QUESTIONS: 1) What kind of foundation is necessary to begin a Supplier Certification program? 2) What does a Total Quality Control Charter contain?

ANSWERS: 1) In one sense, Jim Kvek, manager of the Total Quality Control Department at Ricoh (an electronic equipment manufacturer), is trying to work himself out of a job. Kvek says that when his company first began to consider a certification program, they quickly realized that they were "putting the cart before the horse."

"You can't begin a program in the middle," he adds, "so we went back to the beginning. We began by reviewing our quality assurance procedures and by implementing an internal program of Total Quality Control. We aimed for total involvement from everybody in the company. My job is to transfer the responsibility for quality from the TQC Department to the whole company."

Kvek says that he effects this transference by communicating goals through pamphlets to employees and new hires and through committees composed of people from different levels of the organization.

"I am not here to give presentations, " Kvek says. "I am here to assist project teams and provide them with the tools they need to understand and solve problems. Of course, training and education is one of the most valuable tools I can provide."

All of Ricoh's efforts at establishing a foundation for Supplier Certification have been greatly aided by the complete support of top management. Much of the California plant's top management worked at Ricoh in Japan when the company won the prestigious **DEMING PRIZE** for quality control, the top award in Japan and arguably the world. Kvek points out that there was no need to "go through a convincing process."

2) Much of the company's effort revolves around a Total Quality Control Charter. It defines TQC as:

> "... an environment in which all of us accept the responsibility of our *customers* as that of our own; a customer is any internal or external individual affected by our actions."

Furthermore, the definition states that TQC is an "attitude reflecting teamwork, integrity, honesty and a commitment to statisfy all customer needs." It also states that TQC is "involved in all aspects of company activities."

The adopted philosophy is that each step in a process is the previous step's customer.

As for the goals of the TQC Charter, they can be summed up as achieving the acceptance and practice of TQC by the entire company as well as the recognition that it is everybody's responsibility to contribute ideas, effort, time and service in support of these objectives. More specifically, the charter contains the following goals:

BUSINESS GOALS

Schedules being met
Improved quality
Reduction in rework
Attainment of optimum product cost
Lower inventory
Supplier certification program
Improved customer satisfaction

PERSONAL GOALS

Improved employee morale
Lower turnover rate
Fewer absentees

INTERNAL GOALS

Improved profitability
Meeting Sector goals

This charter also outlines the responsibilities of the TQC Department. As Kvek stated earlier, one of the principal responsibilites of his department is to provide training in Total Quality Control. The document also cites another responsibility as finding a consultant whose "ideology is compatible" with that of the company. Ricoh selected Professionals for Technology (Pro-Tech) in Plantsville, CT, because their skill base was compatible with the company, particularly Pro-Tech's knowledge of both American and Pacific Rim companies. The duty of this consultant is to organize all the training courses about TQC.

The charter includes the means by which Project Teams or employees are to be recognized for outstanding contributions to the TQC project. This is important, the charter says, because it "provides a continuous, company-wide forum for recognizing and publicly thanking employees for their extraordinary perception, dedication and action in responding to the business needs of our customers, both internal and external."

It is clear that Ricoh has recognized as well that Supplier Certification not only rests on a foundation of Total Quality Control, but also on a base of respect and open communication with their people. Kvek wants the people at Ricoh to build quality into their work. He hopes that project teams eventually become second nature at the company. Then he will know he has done his job right.

As a footnote, Ricoh has also set a corporate goal of winning the Baldridge Award for quality excellence. This award, named for the late Secretary of Commerce, is the American version of the Deming Prize.

AWD LTD.
Dunstable, England

QUESTIONS: 1) What questions do you ask a potential supplier? 2) What kind of format do you use for a supplier appraisal? 3) What are some of the requirements of Supplier Certification and a supplier agreement?

ANSWERS: 1) AWD, Ltd., an automotive parts manufacturer, has woven together a comprehensive Supplier Certification program. The supplier questionnaire, says Senior Purchase Engineer I.W. Burgess, is the form sent to potential suppliers in order to assess whether they meet AWD's requirements. The form shown here gives some of the questions which the company deems important:

AWD LTD SUPPLIER QUESTIONNAIRE

1.   NAME OF COMPANY:

2.   COMPANY PERSONNEL
     (Please include organization charts)

3.   DETAILS OF FINANCIAL STRUCTURE AND AFFILIATIONS WITH OTHER COMPANIES.
     (Please include copy of latest Annual Report)

4.   ANNUAL TURNOVER:

5.   DATE COMPANY ESTABLISHED:

6.   SIZE OF PLANT IN SQUARE FEET:

7.   PLANT LIST:

8.   TOTAL NUMBER OF EMPLOYEES:

9.   ANNUAL LABOR TURNOVER:

10. HAVE YOU:
    (A) A SEPARATE QUALITY CONTROL DEPT.?
    (B) A LABORATORY?
    (C) ADEQUATE FACILITIES FOR TESTING TO
        MEET OUR SPECIFICATIONS?

11. HAVE YOU:
    (A) YOUR OWN TOOL ROOM?
    (B) TOOL DESIGN FACILITIES?
    (C) TOOL TRYOUT FACILITIES?
    (D) WHAT PERCENTAGE OF YOUR TOOLING
        IS SUB-CONTRACTED?

2) Providing that the received information from the supplier satisfies AWD's critical requirements, a full appraisal visit is then scheduled at the supplier's plant. The appraisal team consists of a representative from Purchasing Engineering, S.Q.A. and Laboratory departments. This team completes a Supplier Appraisal form. The example shown below is a partial listing of its components:

AWD LTD SUPPLIER APPRAISAL

SUPPLIER:
ADDRESS:
TEL NO:
DATE OF VISIT:
PERSONNEL INTERVIEWED:
PERSONNEL AWD:
RECOMMENDATION:

	FULL APPROVAL	PARTIAL APPROVAL	NIL
Purch. engineering	[ ]	[ ]	[ ]
S.Q.A.	[ ]	[ ]	[ ]
Engineering	[ ]	[ ]	[ ]
Laboratory	[ ]	[ ]	[ ]

Suppliers which meet the following requirements are designated as "Certification Approved":

- Minimum Category 4 compliance to S.Q.A.
  general quality standards for purchased materiel.

- Have proven sample and bulk performance
  ascertained from existing quality documentation.

3) The supplier must then submit a "Certificate of Bulk Conformity" each month to cover all conforming parts delivered during the preceding month. At the discretion of a Certification Committee, a supplier who demonstrates satisfactory performance over a 12-month period will only be required to sign an agreement confirming that AWD's quality requirements will be met. The "Certificate of Bulk Conformity" contains the following paragraph:

> We hereby certify that the above mentioned parts/
> materiel have been manufactured, tested and inspected in accordance with the requirements of the
> drawing, documents and specifications current at
> the time of manufacutre, issued by AWD LTD.
> We certify that the said parts/material were found
> to be in conformity herewith.

The Certification Committee is responsible for controlling the list of participating suppliers. It is comprised of Materials Management and Quality Control representatives. A full list of "Certification Approved" sources is retained and updated by Purchase Engineering. This list is then made available to Purchasing Groups, S.Q.A., Laboratory, Product Engineering and Material departments.

A supplier can be removed from the certification system for the following reasons:

- S.Q.A. appraisal at source.
- Quality Assurance and/or Laboratory rejections.
- Initial sample rejections.
- Machining/Assembly/Processing rejections.

All rejections are then investigated by S.Q.A./Laboratory. When a supplier is removed from the program, the Purchase Manager will notify the supplier in writing, giving full reasons for the removal. To be reinstated, a supplier must demonstrate a satisfactory performance over a six-month period. The S.Q.A./Supplier contact group will then resurvey the supplier. Prior to any reinstatement, a meeting is set up between AWD and the supplier by Purchasing. The purpose is to restate the principles of the certification program and obtain the supplier's assurance in writing that it will comply with AWD's requirements.

BAXTER HEALTHCARE INTERNATIONAL
Paramax Systems Division
Irvine, CA

QUESTIONS: 1) Why is Supplier Certification important to a manufacturer of healthcare products? 2) How has the Paramax Division handled the implementaion phase?

ANSWERS: 1) Bob Wielenga, Director of Materials , at the Paramax Systems Division of Baxter Healthcare International manufacturing facility, points out that the healthcare industry is certainly one area where it is clear that 100% quality is absolutetly necessary. The division he works for manufactures a blood chemistry analyzer and the supporting products.

"Quality means conformance to requirements. In the healthcare industry, quality and service to the customer is essential," Wielenga says. "Our products are used in making critical decisions. For that reason alone, we think Supplier Certification is essential."

Wielenga cites the increasing costs incurred by healthcare providers as another reason for a certification program. As hospitals and doctors, for example, find it more expensive to provide medical care, suppliers, such as Paramax, must develop ways to reduce costs without sacrificing quality.

In order to lower these costs, however, the supplier must receive quality goods from their suppliers with zero-defects, on time, and in the right quantity. Again, there can be no sacrifice in quality. Supplier Certification, Wielenga has found, is the means whereby all the links in the supply chain of healthcare can work with each other in the improvement of quality and service.

"The partnership developed through Supplier Certification allows us to continually improve our requirements and to reduce costs," Wielenga says. "It builds long-term relationships in which we can improve quality. Quality in this sense extends beyond meeting print specifications and also includes delivery, quantity, and standard packaging requirements."

2.) Implementation at the Paramax Systems Division has been governed by an internal/external philosophy. Two groups have been formed to work on both of these components. The first group is concerned with internal documentation, process control and paperwork. In other words, those items needed to get a Supplier Certification program off the ground.

The second group works on the supplier side, acquainting them with the foundations of Statistical Process Control, Just-In-Time and Total Quality Control. Paramax firmly believes, however, that no company should attempt to teach these techniques and philosophies to suppliers unless they are using them at their own company.

Together, the two groups are placing the cornerstone for what Steve Barbato, Manufacturing Manager, says will be a "world-class manufacturing organization."

"You cannot achieve this type of an organization," he adds, "without certified suppliers."

CONCLUSION

If there is one common theme to these case studies, it is the importance of coordinating the internal and external components of Supplier Certification. As we repeatedly said: What you expect from your suppliers, you should also expect of your own company. Recently we read, in the November 28 issue of *USA Today,* about a company which epitomizes this approach. Florida Power & Light Company, the article reports, is striving to become the best utility in America. Their desire is so strong that they have even begun a quest to win Japan's Deming Prize for Quality Control.

Since 1983, Florida Power has trained every employee in quality control. *USA Today* reports that 8,600 of its 14,000 employees "were grouped into 1,400 quality circles." The newspaper cites impressive results of Florida Power's internal quality program:

- Lost-time injuries are down 34%.

- Completion of a power plant that was $600 million under budget and finished in six years or less than half the industry average.

- Customer complaints cut in half.

It is this last result which shows us that Florida Power understands Supplier Certification. Its customers, the people and businesses which buy power, are having their requirements met. That is the true test of Supplier Certification.

BIBLIOGRAPHY

Peter L. Grieco, Jr., Michael W. Gozzo, **MADE IN AMERICA:** *The Total Business Concept*, PT Publications, Inc., Plantsville, CT.

Peter L. Grieco, Jr., Michael W. Gozzo, Jerry W. Claunch, **JUST-IN-TIME PURCHASING:** *In Pursuit of Excellence,* PT Publications, Inc., Plantsville, CT.

H. Thomas Johnson, Robert S. Kaplan, **RELEVANCE LOST:** *The Rise and Fall of Management Accounting*, Harvard Business School Press, Boston, MA.

Tom Peters, **THRIVING ON CHAOS:** *Handbook for a Management Revolution*, Knopf, New York, NY.

Armand V. Feigenbaum, **TOTAL QUALITY CONTROL**, McGraw-Hill Book Co., New York, NY.

PRODUCTION AND INVENTORY MANAGEMENT REVIEW and APICS NEWS, Raymond G. Feldman, Editor; Richard D'Alessandro, Publisher; Hollywood, FL.

Lamar Lee, Jr., Donald W. Dobler, **PURCHASING AND MATERIALS MANAGEMENT:** *Text and Cases*, McGraw-Hill Book Co., New York.

PURCHASING MAGAZINE, James P. Morgan, Editor, John F. O'Connor, Publisher, Cahners Publishing Co., Newton, MA.

W. Edwards Deming, **QUALITY, PRODUCTIVITY AND COMPETITIVE POSTION**, MIT Center for Advanced Engineering Study, Cambridge, MA.

HARVARD BUSINESS REVIEW, Theodore Levitt, Editor; James A. McGowan, Publisher; Boston, MA.

Thomas J. Peters, Robert H. Waterman, **IN SEARCH OF EXCELLENCE**, Warner Books, Inc., New York, NY.

Philip B. Crosby, **QUALITY IS FREE**, New American Library, New York, NY.

FORTUNE, Marshall Loeb, Editor, James B. Hayes, Publisher, New York, NY.

TRAFFIC MANAGEMENT, Francis J. Quinn, Editor; Ron Bondlow, Publisher; Cahners Publishing Co., Newton, MA.

MODERN MATERIALS HANDLING, Ray Kulwiec, Editor; William G. Sbordon, Publisher; Cahners Publishing Co., Newton, MA.

INDEX